ESSENTIAL GUIDE TO
LONDON'S RETRO SHOPS

CLIVE DUNKLEY

NEW HOLLAND

First published in 2005 by
New Holland Publishers (UK) Ltd
London • Cape Town • Sydney • Auckland

www.newhollandpublishers.com

Garfield House, 86–88 Edgware Road, London, W2 2EA,
United Kingdom

80 McKenzie Street, Cape Town 8001, South Africa

14 Aquatic Drive, Frenchs Forest, NSW 2086, Australia

218 Lake Road, Northcote, Auckland, New Zealand

ISBN 1 84330 971 8

Publishing Manager: Jo Hemmings
Senior Editor: Charlotte Judet
Design: Gülen Shevki-Taylor
Maps: William Smuts
Production: Joan Woodroffe

Reproduction by Pica Digital Pte Ltd, Singapore
Printed and bound in Singapore by Kyodo Printing Co (Pte) Ltd

contents

IN WITH THE OLD, OUT WITH THE NEW

The future was everywhere back in the 50s and 60s. You could barely open a magazine or turn on the TV without coming across some image of mankind's silver-suited descendants. And if it wasn't the people themselves then it was their Plexiglas homes or nuclear-powered cars. Yet for all the flights of fancy, those post-war illustrations remained emphatically of their time. In the ballrooms of Mars, it seemed, kitten heels would still be de rigueur, whilst inside the space-men's helmets would be familiar Brylcreemed quiffs. Nowadays, as far as many of us are concerned, there are few things more evocative of those particular past decades than their quaint visions of things to come.

Of course, here in the new millennium we're living in the very golden age which all those earlier artists and set-designers were trying to predict. And in hi-tech terms at least we've clearly come a long way. We aren't quite taking day-trips to the stars, but we do have space ships – of a sort – and mobile phones are pretty smart, not to mention 'Playstation 2'. But when it comes to fashion and design who would ever have guessed that in the early 21st century the most up-to-the-minute, utterly contemporary styles in town would be the ones from 40 or 50 years before?

Welcome to the world of retro, where 'old' is the new 'new' and 'then' is well and truly 'now'. Whether it's vintage clothes, classic cars, swing-dance or sixties sofas, ever-growing numbers of people are engaged in a lively dialogue with the not-so-distant past. This passion for all things revitalised and reinvented might even be the defining cultural trend of today. It's certainly the most fun!

The phenomenon is growing so fast that it's not easy to get it all in view. But look behind the myriad ways in which the retro boom is taking shape and there's one thing, more than any other, which seems to have set it all in motion. We're rediscovering the old because we've lost our appetite for the new. In a world of new-improved-formulas and next-big-things, of never-ending overhauls, upgrades and rebrandings we've finally reached the point where the eagerly anticipated and the instantly redundant have become one and the same. And far from coming as a shock, this has brought us a sense of relief – as if we've been cured of some weird compulsion. No longer in thrall to just the latest thing in town, we're free instead to savour the more lasting rewards of things which went before. In a sense, it's the brave old world we hanker after now. Or to borrow a line from Turgenev: 'the rearguard can so easily become the vanguard – all it takes is a change of direction'.

The timing of this about-turn is no coincidence. Drawing a line under the 20th century has helped us to appreciate its legacy, from the timeless fashion templates of Chanel or Mary Quant, to the design triumphs of a bakelite telephone or Fender Strat. And as the calendar charts our progress into a whole new thousand years, it prompts a continuing process of re-evaluation and taking stock.

Ironically, this exploration of the past is helped along by gadgetry which couldn't be more up-to-date. The internet is vastly enriching our relationship with previous decades, and for the first time fans of Texas rockabilly, beaded bags, or the chairs of Verner Panton can share their enthusiasm in a forum to which the whole globe has access. It's no wonder that in today's info-rich, internet-enabled world, ever more people are becoming expert about matters which would previously have seemed arcane. In other words, the distance between marginal and mainstream, as between past and present, is narrowing all the time.

Not just ideas but the vintage items themselves are changing hands more easily as a result of the World Wide Web – witness the success of eBay. The growing trade underlines the time-honoured truth that originals so often boast qualities which aren't so easily reproduced. Take a modern copy of a 50s dress. It might have the same general shape, but will it have all the priceless extras too? - the hidden hooks-and-eyes which guarantee a snug fit, the fabric-covered buttons or the little pocket in the lining for tucking away keys or an emergency lipstick? Best of all, when you've bought vintage, no-one else will turn up to a party in the same outfit!

What we're seeing is the emergence of a whole retro lifestyle, taking many forms and causing a stir of truly international proportions. Vintage clothes are in demand from Hollywood to Harajuku; swing is the thing in New York; and hot-rods are all the rage in Sweden. But the trend has found its most fertile soil right here in London, a city which has mastered the neat trick of being at the cutting-edge – whether for fashion, music or design - whilst also retaining a tremendous respect for the past. It's a place where go-ahead architects go head to head with conservationists, at the same time as its crumblier parts breed new businesses and ideas. Even our youth movements remain bound up with the establishment they oppose (look at the importance of good old British tailoring to Teddy Boys and Mods).

Nowhere is this intoxicating mix of old and new better illustrated than in London's revitalised East End, which is now home to a huge range of mixed-millenia retailers from vintage clothing stores such as 'Rokit' and 'Beyond Retro' to 'Scooter Emporium' and design favourite, 'Two Columbia Road'. Homerton even boasts a unique analogue recording studio much-loved by The White Stripes. But this is just one small part of London's vast retro jigsaw, which spreads out through Islington and Oxford Street, Greenwich, Waterloo and Notting Hill. Camden meanwhile remains a breeding ground for the swanky 'destination shops' of tomorrow, and in The Stables Market there are real treasures to be found: Pop furnishings by Panton, Italian lighting, Scandinavian 70s sideboards, vintage Hawaiian shirts, and even – in person - 60s songster Chris Farlowe, who now does a good line in fifties furniture.

Like any jigsaw, this one has its far-flung corners too, and there's a special excitement about the retro one-offs or tiny enclaves which pepper the outskirts of town. None is more exhilarating than the recently rebuilt Ace Café, which now caters to a whole new generation of bikers, scooterists and hot-rodders, every one of them drawn not only by the building itself but also by the history it represents. A visit to the Ace conjures up that whole vanished culture of which British bikes were once an integral part – an age of ton-ups and fry-ups and Gene and Eddie at 45rpm, all in a two-stroke heaven untroubled by Cortinas or colour TV. Add in the attractions of live music and a decent bacon buttie and as far as I'm concerned this is a World Heritage Site on a par with Stonehenge.

In the pages which follow are details of bars, cafés, tailors, and specialist shops for everything from costume jewellery, vintage guitars, lamps, drums, curtains and tables, to radios, magazines, bikes, shoes and just about every type of clothing one could ever want to wear. But even more than that, the words and pictures in this book are a celebration of all the unique, date-defying delights which make London the retro capital of the world.

When all's said and done, our current exploration of the past is less to do with travelling back in time than about restoring the place of history in our everyday lives. In our pay-as-you-go, pick-and-mix world, the styles and sounds of past decades are all back on the menu. What we do with them is up to us, but there's no good reason why a design which excited us once shouldn't do so again. Who knows, fifty years from now our cars may fly and be nuclear-powered after all - but I wouldn't bet against them having fins.

HOW TO USE THIS BOOK

For the purposes of this book, London has been divided into the following five areas:

- **Central:** With the City to the east and Knightsbridge to the west, retro action in central London is focused around Covent Garden and Charing Cross Road. Marylebone adds a splash of colour too, whilst Hanway Street is a tiny, timeless universe all of its own. Even Oxford Street has some surprises in store, thanks to Top Shop and John Lewis, and the legendary music venue, The 100 Club.
- **West:** Starting in South Kensington, the retro route west leads through Fulham,

Hammersmith, Acton and Ealing and extends as far as distant Hanwell (where you can buy the perfect motorbike to get you back into town). But the area's most compelling port of call will always be Notting Hill, which offers a huge range of world-class shops including some of London's very best for vintage clothing.

- **North:** Camden has long been a centre for retro goodies of every type, and the sheer number of dealers in and around NW1 makes 'North' the largest section of this book. Furniture and design are especially strong at Chalk Farm's Stables Market, with clothes and records coming close behind. Not so far away in NW8 is Alfie's Antique Centre, home to a remarkable number of specialists in everything from posters and beaded dresses to fantastic Italian lights.

- **East:** In recent years Brick Lane and Columbia Road have become top destinations for all fans of mid-century style – whether design or clothing — and Pellicci's café in nearby Bethnal Green offers the ideal spot to rest the legs. Beyond E1 and E2 other gems are dotted about further east, from Homerton and Walthamstow, to the sublime 'Elvis Shop' in Manor Park.

- **South:** South of the river, London's retro connoisseurs head mainly for the hotspots of Waterloo and Greenwich, fast becoming the perfect choice for a 'vintage' day out. Looking further afield, an irresistible case for venturing beyond the usual postcodes is made by the Battersea-born but now Surrey-based 'Dreamcars', home to a superb collection of American classics.

Within each area, the types of retro shop are classified by the goods they sell:

- **Nosh ☜:** Cafés, bars and music venues, chosen for their classic post-war interiors, pre-decimal charm, or hip-shaking retro playlists.
- **Pad ☝:** Mid-century design stores, selling original items of furniture and lighting from the thirties to the eighties. Also includes ceramics, magazines, hi-fi equipment, jukeboxes, posters, and even a black-and-white photo studio.
- **Threads ☝:** Vintage clothing from the Jazz Age onwards, both men's and women's, and for all tastes and budgets from couture to street fashion. Tastefully accompanied by costume jewellery, shoes, bags, a host of other accessories, and even some authentic old-school tattoos.
- **Tunes ♫:** Rare, classic and reissued vinyl along with CDs, books and memorabilia covering rock, pop, blues, jazz, country, garage, punk, soul, reggae, psychedelia, exotica, latin and swing from the thirties to the eighties. Also includes vintage guitar and drum shops, as well as a couple of analogue recording studios.
- **Wheels ☼:** Dealers in vintage scooters, classic American cars, and Golden Age British bikes, further revved up by the addition of a unique Kustom Kar bodyshop.

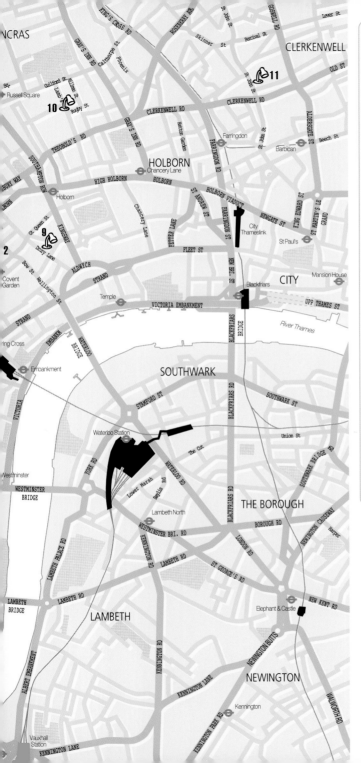

central

central: nosh

The very centre of town boasts some of London's finest retro watering holes, from old-school eateries with classic interiors to down-home venues for late night drinks and music. You can even learn some swing-dance steps for cutting a rug on the floor.

MARYLEBONE

This Marylebone institution has its origins in the nineteenth century, when the first Mr Rothe left Saxony for late Victorian London. He brought with him a love for the kind of fine, prepared foods that were plentiful back home but as yet relatively unknown to his new neighbours. An idea was duly born, and in 1900 the capital saw the opening of one of its very first delicatessens. The shop was a success, though the concept was not one that many rushed to copy; even by the 1920s there was still only a handful of specialists in 'continental comestibles', and the Rothe family were delivering their rye loaves to addresses as far away as Hampstead.

> ## Paul Rothe & Sons
>
> Address: 35 Marylebone Lane, W1
> Hours: Mon–Fri 08:00–18:00, Sat 12:00–18:00
> Telephone: 020 7935 6783
> Tube: Bond Street
> Bus: 6, 7, 10, 13, 73, 113, 139, 189

After the war, the addition of seating gave the place more the feel of a cafeteria, and the store today is largely unchanged from its last major refit in the 1950s. Smart new tables and chairs with fashionable chrome frames were installed in 1955, and a couple more were added in the 1960s when the original manufacturer was still able to produce a perfect match. All have been accommodating diners ever since, and the current Mr Rothe is able to be so precise about the dates because he still has the receipts!

Centre of attention remains the deli cabinet, dispensing homemade houmous and kümmel cheese, along with Polish kabanos, Hungarian salami and a range of more familiar fare. For eating in or taking away, the menu offers all of the above

Home to London's Lindyhoppers since 1942, the legendary
100 Club (see next page)

in sandwich form, and in a variety of breads including the famed Ukrainian rye. Hot food includes jacket potatoes and popular soups such as chicken and ham or minted pea. Around the walls are shelves laden with all sorts of daily provisions, from jams and pasta to packets of tea, whilst the festive season provides an annual opportunity to celebrate in style with a big show of stollen, lebkuchen and other sticky treats. Outside, just to the left of the main shop front, is a charming display of family history with some wonderfully evocative photos of the Rothes and their produce in days gone by. Don't miss!

OXFORD STREET

To paraphrase Chuck Berry, "Hail! Hail! The 100 Club!". Of London's many live music venues this simple Oxford Street basement is the most evocative, boasting appearances by some of the greatest performers of all time. For what it's been, for what it is, and for its unique life-affirming spirit the club is the very emblem of all that is great about the capital's contribution to popular musical culture.

The 100 Club

Address: 100 Oxford St, W1
Hours: Times vary, but open most nights from 19.30 'til around 24.00, later on Fri & Sat
Telephone: 020 7636 0933
Web: www.the100club.co.uk
Tube: Tottenham Court Rd
Bus: 7, 10, 55, 73, 176, 390

Opened as a restaurant in 1942 its live jazz policy saw Glenn Miller take the stage, and before long war-time audiences were escaping the doodlebugs above for a night's jitterbugging down below. The 50s saw visits from jazz and blues greats such as Louis Armstrong, Muddy Waters and BB King, whilst the 60s British R&B explosion sent the likes of the Who, Animals, Pretty Things and Kinks all following in their wake. The club's remarkable openness to new directions was never more apparent than in 1976, when it hosted the first ever punk festival, offering a line-up of then unknown acts such as the Sex Pistols, Clash, Damned, Buzzcocks and Banshees – all on one bill! New music has continued to feature in recent years, from African township jive to early gigs by Suede and Oasis, and even the up-and-coming Indie bands of today are still as likely to make their name here as anywhere else.

Phew! Just think about it: from Glenn Miller to Oasis and everything in between. And yet, for somewhere so steeped in history, the place remains both thrillingly alive and blissfully attitude-free. Everything about the 100 Club is inclusive and democratic, from its 'everyone on board' lack of dress code to its sensible bar prices, basic furniture, and even the unreconstructed loos. That's why we love it! It's an honest deal in a world of scams, where the management measure their success not by the number of stretch limos parked outside but by the number of happy, sweaty people who exit nightly after a damned good workout on the floor (or at the bar).

What you'll actually hear depends on the day of the week, with many nights earmarked for

50s seating at Rothe & Sons

popular, long-running clubs. Mondays are home to 'Stompin', the flagship event of the London Swing Dance Society and hosted by Simon Selmon since 1987. Newcomers to swing can enjoy an early evening lesson and are always welcome on the floor, whilst lifelong Lindy Hoppers treat the rest of us to some jaw-dropping displays. Add in a superb live band to keep the tempo hot and it's no wonder that 'Stompin' is such a wild success. Fridays and Saturdays see a change of mood with funk, latin, jazz and even hip-hop on the bill, whilst soul fans congregate for the legendary '6Ts Northern All Nighters' which Ady Croasdell has been running since the 70s. In any month's full line-up, music lovers of every stripe are sure to find something to tickle their fancy. Doors open at around 7.30 and bands are usually on stage by 9.15. No need to leave early as night buses run right outside. Absolutely 100 per cent!

PICCADILLY

As I write, the Grim Reaper of Redevelopment is threatening to do away with the unique, glorious and indomitable New Piccadilly. Along with the East End's 'Pellicci', this is one of a tiny handful of London cafés to have survived intact since the genre's post-war glory days. Owner Lorenzo has lived in Denman Street since he was a boy, and remembers his father taking over the old Café Roche before transforming it into the state-of-the-art New

New Piccadilly Café

Address: 8 Denman St, W1
Hours: Times vary, but usually 12:00–20:30 every day
Telephone: 020 7437 8530
Tube: Piccadilly Circus
Bus: 14, 19, 38

Enjoy it while you can, the priceless interior of the New Piccadilly Café

Piccadilly in 1957. When it opened, just a few years after the end of rationing, there were queues outside as customers relished the opportunity of eating out in style. Motorcycles could park right outside, and for a while in the 1960s the café became the favoured central London haunt of the kick-start crowd. A management decision to remove the jukebox resulted in a full-blown riot as disaffected greasers vented their feelings in a barrage of rocks and dustbin lids. Ah, those were the days!

Despite the biker incident, the interior today is exactly as it was in the 1950s, apart from a few extra posters or flowers. Nearest the front are some well used but irreplaceable swivel stools in jazzy yellow and black – perfect for a quick milkshake. Behind them, the dining room is a period picture with parallel rows of yellow formica tables attended by wooden bench seats. Other fixtures to note are the perfect hourglass wall lights, reminding us that in the 1950s even the lights had waists.

As little altered as the surroundings is a menu that remains firmly focused on trad dishes, especially when it comes to comforting, custard-covered puds. Perhaps the only significant change has been among the customers. The old school Englishman demanding his mixed grill and cuppa is something of a dying breed it seems, and the café these days caters to a very international crowd. Apparently, the only way for redevelopment to be postponed is for the economic climate to worsen. To which we can only say: never has a recession looked so good! Get there now, and enjoy this priceless piece of history before it's gone forever.

PIMLICO

The year 1946 was a very fine one in several respects: it brought us the first Cannes Film Festival, the creation of the bikini and, to slightly more localized acclaim, the opening of Pimlico's Regency Café. The area has changed a lot since then, but fortunately for us this traditional British eatery has kept things pretty much as they were.

The black-tiled façade and white-

Regency Café

Address: 17–19 Regency St, SW1
Hours: Mon–Fri 07:00–14:30 &
16:00–19:30, Sat 07:00–12:00
Telephone: 020 7821 6596
Tube: Pimlico
Bus: 2, 36, 185, 436

lettered name perfectly embody the no-nonsense yet stylish modernism that so suited the post-war mood. Inside is mostly monochrome too, though softened by

Full English modernism in Pimlico

gingham half-height curtains and the matching sea-green clapboard around the counter. Only the original bench-type seats have gone, giving way to fixed plastic units in the 1960s. The one other change to note is less a physical than a social one. Where the café was once split into separate blue- and white-collar areas it now forms one happy whole, though the preponderance of yellow safety jackets suggests more a takeover than a merger.

So great is the morning demand that pre-buttered bread waits heaped in baskets, ready to make the perfect man-sized sarnie. Meanwhile the dining room fills with a hubbub of jokes, politics and last night's football results, over which booms the roll-call of incoming orders: 'mushroom omelette', 'double egg and chips' or 'bacon, bubble and tomato' (yes, please!). At the centre of all this activity are owners Marco and Claudia, who have enormous respect for their customers, their food, and the little corner of culinary history they've looked after for nigh on twenty years. Service with a smile, the chips are homemade, and the 'daily specials' are legend; the steak pie especially has a huge fan club, with late-arriving diners mortified to learn that the last piece has been sold. The good news is that Marco has recently made a point of tracking down the most gigantic new pie dish in the hope of satisfying demand. I think we should take that as a challenge!

SOHO

The Blues Bar, as it's commonly known, has been around over ten years, but has the lived-in look of a survivor from the fifties. Picture a classic southern juke joint somehow uprooted from New Orleans or Beale St, Memphis and parked a few blocks south of Oxford Circus. If that sounds incongruous then no one seems to have noticed, as the place fills nightly with one of the liveliest, friendliest, good-time crowds in London. The overall effect is so convincing that it can sometimes

Ain't Nothin' But...

Address: The Blues Bar, 20 Kingly St, Soho, W1
Hours: Mon–Wed 18:00-01:00, Thurs 18:00–02:00, Fri/Sat 12:00-03:00
Telephone: 020 7287 0514
Web: www.aintnothinbut.co.uk
Tube: Oxford Circus
Bus: 3, 6, 12, 13, 15, 23, 88, 94, 139, 159, 453

All-time greats assembled at The Blues Bar

be quite a shock emerging at 1 a.m. to find the back of Liberty's rather than the night skies of Louisiana.

Early evening, the playlist is a mix of blues and early R&B, mostly featuring artists whose names begin with Howlin', T-Bone, Hound Dog or Lightnin'. An emphasis on up-tempo rockin' sounds sets the stage for the live acts, who usually start their set at around 9.30 p.m. Over the years the postage stamp of a stage has played host to a huge range of performers, from local young bloods such as Big Joe Louis to visiting US legends. Seating is a mix of banquettes and solid wooden chairs, though all are snapped up quickly and regulars are used to standing at the bar.

If you think this all adds up to a bloke-ish, beard and beer-belly sort of place, then you'd be wrong. The Blues Bar is extremely female friendly and is a popular choice for after-work drinks, which range from real ale (Adnams) to bourbon and tequila. The food is pretty good too, 'especially the meatballs' – or so said Tony and Linda, my new friends for the evening on my last visit (it's that sort of place!). The midweek late licence has probably been responsible for more than its fair share of morning-after 'sick notes', and on Fridays and Saturdays chucking-out time isn't until 3 a.m. For latest info on gigs and special events, keep an eye on the web site. Bands who fancy having a go should contact the manager, Rob, or turn up for one of the 'open mic' sessions. Let the good times roll.

TOTTENHAM COURT ROAD

Bradley's is the kind of place that shouldn't work: it's tiny, things keep breaking, you can barely get into the cellar... and that's not what *I* think, it's the view of the owner! Mark has been running this legendary bar for around four years, and has no doubt that what makes it such a storming success is its clientèle, who are as diverse a mix as you're ever likely to encounter. Bands come here for a pre-gig drink, and jostle for space with television

Bradley's Spanish Bar

Address: 42–44 Hanway Street, W1
Hours: Mon-Sat 12:00–23:00, Sun 15:00–22:30
Telephone: 020 7636 0359
Tube: Tottenham Court Road
Bus: 10, 73, 390

types, journalists, backpackers, record-shop owners and Kevin the stockbroker who barely speaks English but always brings the staff presents when he's in town.

The bohemian atmosphere is supercharged by the lack of space, making this one of those rare venues where conversations spill over in all directions and new friends are made in an instant. Providing a suitable soundtrack is a much-loved vinyl-playing jukebox that has been relieving regulars of their coins since the 1970s. Mark likes to change the forty-fives from time to time, but always makes sure there's a stock of classics from the Kinks and Hendrix to the Undertones, assorted 1950s crooners and even Glenn Miller.

Apart from its customers and its sounds, Bradley's scores highest in my book for its marvellously unreconstructed interior, dating back at least to the 1960s if not before (no one seems quite sure).

The beating heart of Hanway Street

From the bullfight posters to the Moorish ironwork, the décor evokes a time when Spain was about as exotic a destination as the English mind could cope with. Add in a smattering of red plush and some subterranean cubby-holes to lurk in, and you have just the sort of haunt one would have gone to after the premier of *Blow Up*.

Look out, too, for the photograph of William Bradley, original proprietor and first President of the 'Hanway Club' long before the war. For whistle-wetting there's Cruz Campo and San Miguel on tap, and even if José, famed barman for 30-plus years, is no longer pulling the pints, his spirit lives on in this cheap, cheerful and charming home-from-home. And by the way, Bradley's is unlikely to suffer a 'revamp' soon as there's a 'no decorating' clause in the lease!

Covent Garden's 'Tom Tom' has long been a champion of classic design, and is now joined by memorably named *Eatmyhandbagbitch* as well as other enthusiasts in Marylebone, Clerkenwell and Bloomsbury.

CLERKENWELL

Flin Flon's shop layout is more remarkable than most; the ground floor has been removed to create a double-height space, further individualized by plywood-clad walls. Customers entering at street level thus have a bird's-eye view of the stock before descending the stairs to take a closer look. What they find is a characterful mix of Scandinavian design, mostly mid-century originals with a few contemporary items for good measure. Major-league Danes such as Wegner, Jacobsen and Kjorsgaard are represented by their carefully crafted chests of drawers and tables, as well as chairs with curving backs, angled seats and sinuous arm-rests, all made from the highest quality wood. But what makes Flin Flon really special is its emphasis on the unique style legacy of Finland.

Flin Flon

Address: 138 St. John St, EC1
Hours: Thurs/Fri 12:00–18:00, Sat 12:00–16:00
Telephone: 020 7253 8849
Web: www.flinflon.co.uk
Tube/rail: Farringdon
Bus: 153

First and foremost this means Alvar Aalto, whose pre-war furniture creations in patented 'bent' birch embodied to perfection the modernist ideal. But here, too, are equally iconic pieces by Yrjo Kukkapuro, whose Karuselli swivel chair from 1964 was recently chosen as the 'best design of the century' by Terence Conran. For ceramics, Finns since the 1940s have looked to the work of Kaj Franck, who came to prominence with his Kilta mix-and-match tableware and whose pieces decorate several of the shop's natural, clean-lined surfaces. Likewise the glasses, teapots and assorted everyday objects by Timo Sarpaneva have long had a valued place in Finnish homes, and a good selection – new and vintage – can be found here. Completing the picture are the marvellous Marimekko fabrics, of which owner

Explore the rich style legacy of Finland, from Aalto to Moomintrolls, at Flin Flon

Marianna has a superb collection from the 1950s onwards, many of the patterns having never been reissued. And if this embarrassment of riches isn't enough to prompt serious thoughts of a one-way ticket to Helsinki, then perhaps the Moomintroll mugs will do the trick.

It all adds up to a distinctive take on the Nordic contribution to interior style. Moreover, everything is eminently usable, and would fit easily in most homes. My favourite was the Aalto high chair, proving that even the most practical objects can benefit from world-class design – and what better start in life for the lucky user?

COVENT GARDEN

When a feature in *Radio Times* extols the virtues of Charles Eames over Chippendale, there can no longer be any doubting the ascendancy of post-war design. Interest has been growing steadily over the last five or 10 years, during which time Eatmyhandbagbitch, (or Handbag for short) has been at the crest of the wave.

Eatmyhandbagbitch

Address: 37 Drury Lane, WC2
Hours: Mon–Sat 10:00-18:00
Telephone: 020 7836 0830
Web: www.eatmyhandbagbitch.co.uk
Tube: Covent Gdn/Holborn
Bus: 1, 59, 68, 91, 168, 171, 188, 243

Owners George and Georgina recently traded up from their shop in Brick Lane to a smart new gallery in Covent Garden. They also have a prestigious concession at Selfridge's, where many of the smaller or less expensive items tend to be displayed. On offer is a huge range of classic designs in furniture, lighting, tableware and ceramics, including all the major-league names – Panton, Sottsas, and Robin Day – as well as lesser-known figures such as Mendini and La Pietra. Most items are original, though some are modern limited editions, such as the lovely Joe Colombo wine glasses designed in the mid-1960s: these have a short, off-centre stem so you can grip them between finger and thumb whilst holding a cigarette in the same hand (try selling *those* to a New York restaurant!). Also in the mix are out-of-the-ordinary appliances including a portable colour television by Sanyo – the first to be commercially produced – and Siemens radios made to resemble dice. Although much of the stock is from Italy or Scandinavia, George's current favourites include some British pieces, such as Ernest Race's folding plywood chairs made for P&O cruise liners, or one of A.J. Milne's chairs from the Festival of Britain – originally made for the terrace, most of these were unceremoniously dumped when the festival ended, and only a tiny handful still exist today.

Demand can be influenced by media coverage or big events, and a major retrospective of Whitefriars glassware prompted many new converts to seek out examples of 'Drunken Bricklayers' and other trademark designs. Overall, the general uptrend in prices continues apace, as is best illustrated by those textbook Charles Eames' chairs. Even

60s 'dice' radio by Siemens

before *Radio Times* got in on the act, these had enjoyed a tenfold price rise in as many years. In fact, the Handbaggers find themselves frequently disabusing people of the view that *everything* from the 1960s and 1970s must now be worth a fortune. The truth is, there's an awful lot of junk around. But at least you won't find any here, where all the pieces are expertly chosen as 'antiques of the future'. My only carp is that the vintage televisions don't also pick up period programmes: isn't there some kind of set-top box I can buy?

This book would not be complete without mention of the unique enterprise that is Mathmos. Now a leading manufacturer of all sorts of fun and innovative lighting, the company will always have a place in the annals of design history for having brought us the original 'Astro Lava Lamp' in 1963. Founder and inventor Edward Craven Walker took his inspiration from a curious egg-timer, and spent no fewer than 10 years perfecting the process that was to bring us those hypnotic and ever-mutating dollops of wax we all know and love today.

Mathmos

Address: 8 Shorts Gdns, WC2
Hours: Mon–Sat 10:30–19:00,
Sun 12:30–17:30
Telephone: 020 7836 8587
Web: www.mathmos.com
Tube: Covent Gdn
Bus: 1

Also at: 22–24 Old St, EC1
Hours: Mon–Sat 09:30–18:00
Telephone: 020 7549 2700

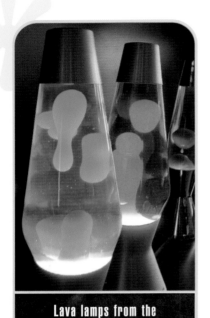

Lava lamps from the original creators

The lamps sold in their millions, but the company's fortunes eventually declined, until in 1989 it was taken over by businesswoman extraordinaire, Cressida Granger. She relaunched it as Mathmos, taking the name from the sentient under-floor soup in Barbarella, and designs new and old are now showcased at the smart HQ in EC1 and at the retail boutique in Covent Garden. Sadly, vintage items aren't on offer, but the '1963 Original' range gives us faithful reproductions. Craven Walker himself bowed out in the year 2000, but he would doubtless have been proud to see his timeless classics still flying off the shelves in the new millennium. Equal testament to his memory is the rate at which Mathmos is now packing its trophy cabinet with awards for brand new creations. As 'Queen' Anita Pallenberg might have said: they are very 'pretty pretty'.

HOLBORN

Rennies is part shop, part gallery, and also more than either: the embodiment of its owners' perspective on art and design, it adds up to a kind of permanent installation for which the title might be 'British Modernism at home, 1920–the present'. Even the building itself – a prettily tiled ex-dairy – exhibits the

Rennies

Address: French's Dairy, 13 Rugby St, WC1
Hours: Tues–Sat 12:00–18:30
Telephone: 020 7405 0220
Web: www.rennart.co.uk
Tube: Holborn/Russell Sq
Bus: 19, 38, 55, 243

same blend of practical design and social history that informs the contents inside.

Illustrated books and enamel badges mingle in the window with ceramics, record covers or silk scarves. In the two rooms beyond, the eclectic collection also embraces furniture, clothing, a marvellous array of posters, and household objects from clocks to cutlery. Such a disparate mix defies all the usual categories, but there is a unifying theme that Paul and Karen Rennie are only too happy to explain.

In a nutshell, the stock brings together the work of British artists who have taken the avant-garde out of the galleries and into people's everyday lives. There are ceramics by Eric Ravilious (for Wedgwood), posters by Paul Nash, furniture by Ambrose Heal, and graphic design by Abram Games, 'Henrion' and Peter Blake. Motivating much of this work is the democratic belief that the best of art and design need not be reserved for an élite, but can be made available to a mass

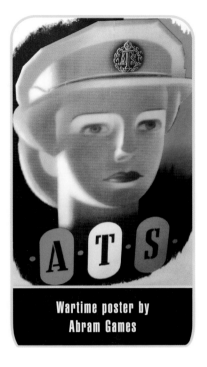

Wartime poster by Abram Games

market, especially with a little help from the latest technology. This view found its apotheosis in the 1951 Festival of Britain, but it continues to influence UK design to the present day. Rennies also aims to show how it inspired a distinctively 'comfy' form of modernism, as likely to be found in the beach hut or the potting shed as in any glitzy bar or grand civic arena.

The shop has the intimate feel of a private home, and it comes as no great surprise to discover that the upper floors are exactly that: the Rennies' living space flows on seamlessly from the showrooms, and is itself a charming – and very comfy – testament to twentieth-century British design. Here one especially sees many of the bold and innovative posters that form the mainstay of the family business.

Prices are as varied as the stock, but start as low as £5 for the badges or £25 for headscarves, rising to £1500 for a gorgeous 'Nimbus' coffee table by Neil Morris, and more still for iconic works of graphic design. The key point to remember is that everything is significantly cheaper than these same artists' output in oils or watercolour. As Paul Rennie points out, this is a place where 'as a collector, you can do something very interesting, but with modest means'.

MARYLEBONE

A s one of Central London's most resurgent areas, Marylebone High Street could hardly qualify as a chic *quartier* without at least one classic design store to its name. This post is more than ably filled by 'Century Design', joint venture of Andrew Weaving (downstairs) and Norma Holland (upstairs), who together preside over an imaginative mix of decorative desirables.

Andrew is an authority on post-war furniture design, having penned several books including the popular *Modern Retro*. His stock majors on architect-designed pieces and modernist icons by the likes of Eames, Nelson and Eero Saarinen, along with enough sympathetic ceramics and fabrics to help furnish a room. Norma meanwhile makes a considerable splash with her line-up of largely Italian items, many of them by designers who are not (yet) household names.

If the likes of Sottsas and Gio Ponti are already in the acknowledged premier league, then at 'Century' we are invited to look instead at someone like Borsani, who from his earliest deco-influenced 1940s creations

Century Designs

Address: 68 Marylebone High St, W1
Hours: Tues–Sat 10:00-18:00 (till 19:00 on Thursday) Sun 12:00-17:00
Telephone: 020 7487 5100
Tube/Rail: Baker St/Regent's Park
Bus: 18, 27, 30, 205, 453

50s flair from Italy

to his futuristic 1970s 'Techno Chair' (typically, £2000) sustained a career of great originality and quality. The items themselves were also very often manufactured to the same high standards as more celebrated designs, and at the very same workshops. Likewise names such as Carlo di Carli, Ico Parisi, Faltini, Albini or Rinaldi may at first read like a 'Serie A' football team, but in fact they represent a whole generation of creative talents as yet relatively unsung outside their own country.

Major pieces on offer at Century include pairs of superb 1950s armchairs in original striped velvet (£1200), as well as all the basics, such as dining tables, sofas and sideboards. Filling the spaces in between are 1960s lights, 1940s mirrored cabinets, Murano glass, and enough general decorative arts to complete the most fastidious retro-modern home-scape. As educational as it is enjoyable, the shop is an 'infotainment' treat.

SOHO

This is the flagship store of what has become a mini chain, with other branches in Oxford and Brighton as well as a second London outlet in Charing Cross Road. All are well known for their varied mix of film and pop ephemera, including stills, postcards, toys and a stock of posters that have helped decorate students' walls for generations. But if it's actual vintage magazines you're after, then Brewer Street is the place to come.

The Vintage Magazine Company

Address: 39–43 Brewer St, Soho, W1
Hours: Mon–Thurs 10:00–20:00, Fri/Sat 10:00–22:00, Sun 12:00–20:00
Telephone: 020 7439 8525
Tube: Piccadilly Circus
Bus: 14, 19, 38

The cavernous basement room is chock full of a whole century's worth of printed matter, much of it arranged by decade, and with signs hanging from the ceiling to help you find your era of choice. If pre-war pulp is your thing then you'll find a satisfyingly lurid copy of *Scarlet Adventuress* (£25) nestling in the '1930s' racks along with various film fanzines, *London Illustrated*, or an occasional super-glamorous *Vogue* – in fact, there are copies of *Vogue* from every decade, right up to the present day. The earlier issues hit the spot, with fabulous photos by Cecil Beaton or Rawlings on almost every page – though with prices known to break the

A century of reading matter

£100 barrier you'll have to be a pretty serious buyer to get your hands on one. Fortunately, post-war numbers still boast top-class images from the likes of Irving Penn and Norman Parkinson, and will set you back more like £25—40.

Of more recent stock, special mention goes to the substantial range of music and street-fashion titles such as *Q*, *Smash Hits* and *The Face*. Elsewhere on the shelves you'll find everything from *Radio Times*, *Harpers* and '*Life*' to *Nova*, and *NME*.

When it comes to gifts, sales are helped by some canny marketing. Each month, mags from exactly 10 years ago (or 20 or 30) are separated out and showcased. This has been a huge hit with people looking for birthday presents – or for something to mark a special anniversary – and the best sellers of all have been the vintage 'top shelf' mags.

Images of all the usual twentieth-century icons are here in number. Cover pics of Marilyn Monroe command the biggest premium, followed closely by The Beatles, Elvis, Sinatra and Audrey Hepburn,.

TOTTENHAM COURT ROAD

Tom Tom is one of a kind, not least because it happens to be 'London's oldest established twentieth-century art and design emporium'. The shop is not huge, consisting of two jam-packed floors in one of those Covent Garden back streets that at first seems to contain only warehouses. But customers – both first-timers and old friends – are drawn to Tom

Tom Tom

Address: 42 New Compton St, WC2
Hours: Tues–Sat 12:00–19:00
Telephone: 020 7240 7909
Web: www.tomtomshop.co.uk
Tube: Tottenham Court Rd
Bus: 1, 14, 19, 24, 29, 38, 176

Tom's doors as if by some tractor beam: spend some time there and you'll be amazed by the steady stream of clued-up aficionados who drop by, from the woman snatching up the very Joe Colombo table lamp she's been after for years, to the student paying homage to a 1950s phonogram, whispering: 'That's the famous "Snow White's Coffin" model, *complete with Plexiglas lid*' (designed by Dieter Rams for Braun, and yours for £550).

The shop was founded by Tommy Roberts, one-time 'Mr Freedom' and owner of original swinging 1960s fashion mecca 'Kleptomania'. When he moved from clothing into post-war design Tommy was a true pioneer, with the vision not so much to spot a trend as virtually to start one! The business is now run by Gary Mitchell, who stays true to Tom Tom's original concept: *'Recycle!'*.

Expect to find classic designs from the 1940s to the 1980s, coupled with a strong line-up of art – much of it contemporary. Peter Blake's Sixties icon 'Babe Rainbow' is joined here by her 2001 companion piece, 'Bobbie Rainbow', whilst around them the fast-changing stock can as easily veer towards the futuristic. But the big names from the immediate post-war years tend to dominate. A George Nelson 'Coconut Chair' designed in 1955 sells for a couple of grand, whilst ever-popular Whitefriars 1960s glassware sells for under a hundred. At the upper end of the price range is a glass-topped coffee table designed by Ringo Starr, with Rolls Royce radiator grills for legs and up for grabs at a trifling £30,000.

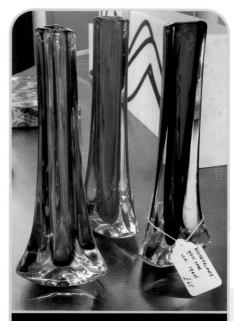

Whitefriars glassware at Tom Tom

Customers range from international galleries to local music types, or the passer-by who simply couldn't resist Jamie Reid's cover art for 'God Save the Queen'. If you're buying for the first time, Gary's advice is to focus on things that haven't been endlessly reproduced and which retain their uniqueness. Come to think of it, a bit like that coffee table…

From the boutiques of Covent Garden to the bright lights of Oxford Street, vintage clothing is now an essential part of London's fashion scene. Those in the know also get their retro chic bespoke at some tip-top Soho tailors

COVENT GARDEN

Just around the corner from Neal Street and Covent Garden's teeming Piazza is the ever-rewarding Blackout II. This is one of those shops where you could walk in naked and emerge hours later with a complete period wardrobe, from hat to boots and everything in-between. The stock includes a sizeable men's selection – about a third of the total – with suits going back to the 1930s, shoes from the 1940s to the 1970s, and a strong all-round showing from the 1950s and 1960s, especially the shirts.

Blackout II

Address: 51 Endell St, WC2
Hours: Mon–Fri 11:00-19:00,
Sat 11:30–18:30
Telephone: 020 7240 5006
Web: www.blackout2.com
Tube: Covent Gdn
Bus: 1

But the real goodies are reserved for the ladies. Owner, Roz, is a well known authority on handbags, and she always carries a superb range: beautifully displayed on tiered shelves all around the main ground-floor room you'll find everything, from dinky 1950s numbers in solid lucite with sculpted sides and carved lids, to delicate clutch-bags encrusted with tiny coloured beads. There's something for every taste, and any one of them would look as good in an after-hours bar as at the Opera House. Some even come with matching pairs of shoes, which is something you almost never see outside a vintage magazine. To explain how this unique trick is made possible, we first need to take a trip downstairs…

The large basement room would, in any case, be a 'must-see' for its rails of fabulous dresses, from 1950s frou-frou to 1960s chic by way of sequins, minis and classic floral prints. But it also boasts what must surely be London's most remarkable collection of women's vintage shoes. The variety of styles is enormous, with many pairs boasting exquisite decorative touches such as patterned tooling, little bows,

Blackout is a treasure-trove of quality vintage clothing, from hats to heels and everything in between buckles, coloured leather flowers or two-tone toes. What's even more surprising is that inside most of them you'll find the same manufacturer's name: Joseph LaRose.

For 50 years, until 1999, Mr Larose sold shoes in and around Jacksonville, Florida. Throughout that time he was always keen to realize new possibilities of shoe design, however fantastic, from experiments with heels and soles to using materials such as jewels and fur, and all in a range of colours that left no part of the spectrum unexplored. Clients included major names from the showbiz world such as Joan Crawford and Jayne Mansfield, and some of his more fanciful creations now fetch big dollars at auction. But what is most incredible of all, is that over the decades he held on to all his unsold inventory, until by the time of his death he had a collection numbering hundreds of thousands of pairs, all stored away and neatly labelled like a one-stop history of post-war women's footwear.

Since this treasure trove first came to light some parts of it have been sold off, and London's shoe lovers have Roz to thank for being the lucky purchaser of several thousand pairs (with matching accessories). In other words, if you don't see what you're after on the shelves, then just ask, as there's a *lot* more where those came from. Prices are reasonable too, with even the amazing sets of shoes and bags going for around £95, whilst pairs on their own sell for £40—60.

No doubt about it, this is vintage shoe heaven, so come and give your feet a unique treat.

S hops in the West End come and go so fast there's barely time for the paint to dry. So three cheers for Cenci, which has been a fixture on Monmouth Street since 1986, and offers a huge range of clothing and accessories all dished up with the kind of enthusiasm you wish you could bottle and take home. Owners Didi and Massimo are passionate about what they do, and have real pride in their stock. Ask to see a few more pairs of cufflinks or a different style of brooch, and

Cenci

Address: 31 Monmouth St, WC2
Hours: Mon–Sat 11:00-18:00
Telephone: 020 7836 1400
Tube: Covent Gdn/Leicester Sq
Bus: 1

Also at: 4 Nettlefold Place, Knight's Hill, SE27
Hours: By appointment
Telephone: 020 8766 8564

before you know it they'll be eagerly producing huge piles of boxes and cases chock full of vintage treasures. They're just as keen to point out all the details that make something dear to their heart, whether it's the quality of the wool used in

1950s knitwear, or the intricate hand-loomed design of a 1960s shirt.

Much of the stock is Italian in origin, which accounts for its often chic and elegant 'Roman Holiday' sort of feel. US-sourced accessories add a touch of glitz or a bold highlight where you want it. There are braces, shoes, luggage, umbrellas with Perspex handles (£30—45) and a wide selection of vintage specs, including those lovely sunglasses with the green lenses (£40/50). Menswear is particularly strong, with

The perfect 60s bag — and the whole wardrobe to go with it — at Cenci

a huge selection of 1940s ties, gabardine shirts (£12—26), and light, woollen 1960s sports tops that would look as good on the beach as on the scooter. For the daring, there's a fab selection of pre-lycra swimwear, including trunks with belts and zips (think Burt Lancaster in *From Here to Eternity*).

The range of womenswear is equally impressive. Ever-popular 1950s cardigans are here in number, as are ski-jumpers, suits and scarves, whilst the rails of dresses include something for every occasion, from proms and cocktails to a summer's stroll in the park. Deserving of a special mention are the bags, Didi's current favourite being a versatile little marvel from the 1940s (£175): its reversible outer casing can be switched from black velvet to shimmering brocade, whilst the inner section can be removed altogether to form an elegant clutch bag. Glamorous 1950s designs in ice-cream shades are also a hit right now, especially the ones in vinyl or moulded plastic. And I mustn't forget the hats, which range from natty noir-ish confections in fur and net to wedding-friendly numbers with bows and veils. Delightful!

The Pop Boutique is just one outlet for the thriving Manchester-based Vintage Clothing Company, who also sell through no less a store than Top Shop in Oxford Street. Owner Richard Free has been in the business for more than 20 years, and has played a leading role in bringing vintage into the mainstream. What's more, he remains as keen as ever to share his passion.

Pop Boutique

Address: 6 Monmouth St, WC2
Hours: Mon–Sat 11:00–19:00, Sun 12:00–17:00
Telephone: 020 7497 5262
Web: www.pop-boutique.com
Tube: Covent Gdn/Leicester Sq
Bus: 1

The company operates on a massive scale. Clothes are imported by the ton, before being farmed out to stores and wholesalers. Monmouth Street typically receives three deliveries a week, and each one numbers around 300–400 items. The prices are low, and the stock turns over at a breathtaking rate, making this the kind of shop where it really pays to 'pop' back on a regular basis. Both the affordability and the clothes themselves appeal to a younger, good-time crowd who know how to look their best on a budget, whether they're off to the dance floor, college library or pub.

Shirts average around £12 and dresses £20, whilst the range as a whole extends to shoes, belts, ethnic blouses, coats, knits and more. Much of the stock is from the 1960s and 1970s, with occasional older pieces when they're available at the right price. Stand-outs such as psychedelic dresses, peasant tops and cute cotton summer frocks complement staples such as jeans and T-shirts. Perennial best-sellers are the trendy shoulder bags emblazoned with logos of sports companies or long-defunct airlines, which seem to have become the Louis Vuitton of the

Chart-toppers at 'Pop'

under-30s. The company's own versions, with Mod-inspired 'Pop' design, can be seen all over town (and in Manchester). Stylists and designers are always dropping by to keep in touch with what's 'in', and the shop really prides itself on how fast it picks up on new trends.

For those who like their sitting room to complement their wardrobe, there's even a selection of glassware, ceramics and vintage telephones.

Since 1982, Rokit has been a familiar name to fans of retro styling in Camden and Brick Lane, but the 'arrival' of vintage has surely had no greater proof than the opening of the new flagship store in Covent Garden. The huge space just a short walk from the Piazza is chock-full of everything from jeans and T-shirts to swanky evening wear, and competes head on with all the nearby big-name designer outlets.

Quality control and attractive presentation are hallmarks of the Rokit approach. Customers are also helped by the careful zoning of the clothes, which are all clearly grouped by size. Menswear figures highly, and goes beyond 70s flares and patterned shirts into the more rarefied territory of 50s gabardine jackets and those fab chunky cardies with knitted designs of ships, horses and bears (all originals, £25-50). Girls can choose from an enormous range of dresses, including huge selections from the 50s and 60s, along with tops, net petticoats and big-buttoned tailored coats (£25). And both sexes tend to fight over the vintage Western shirts, Big E Levis and leather flying jackets.

Rokit prides itself on both its sheer variety and its razor sharp fashion sense. Stock can change in an instant to accommodate the latest 'must have' essential, as when the recent craze for cowboy boots prompted a wall-full of them on the backlit shelves at Covent Garden. Each of the stores has a slightly different focus, but all offer a well-chosen selection catering to pretty much every taste and budget.

Rokit

Address: 41 Shelton St, WC2
Hours: Mon–Sat 10.00–19.00 ('til 20.00 on Thrs), Sun 11.30-18.00
Telephone: 020 7836 6547
Web: www.rokit.co.uk
Tube: Covent Gdn
Bus: 1

Also at: 101-107 Brick Lane, E1
Telephone: 020 7375 3864

225 Camden High St, NW1
Telephone: 020 7267 3046

23 Kensington Gdns, Brighton
Telephone: 01273 672053

'Starship', 49 The Arches, Stables Market, Chalk Farm Rd, NW1

Vintage glamour and cutting-edge chic at Rokit

KNIGHTSBRIDGE

Glasses have long outgrown any kind of merely functional status, and in recent years they have become the hippest, most streetwise of accessories: now, everybody wants to wear them, and no self-respecting wardrobe would be complete without at least a pair or two of ice-cool shades. Cutler & Gross is a name already much revered in the fashion world for its stylish contemporary designs, but in 2003 the shop in Knightsbridge Green was joined by a sister store, just a few doors down, selling only vintage pieces. Remarkably, none of the items on sale has ever been worn before, but all are mint and boxed, making this a true one-of-a-kind.

The venture evolved from the long-time passion of co-owner Tony Gross, who has been collecting eyewear since the 1960s. Newcomers to the scene soon

Cutler & Gross Vintage

Address: 7 Knightsbridge Green, SW1
Hours: Mon–Sat 09:30–18:00
Telephone: 020 7590 9995
Web: www.cutlerandgross.com
Tube: Knightsbridge
Bus: 9, 10, 14, 52, 74, 414

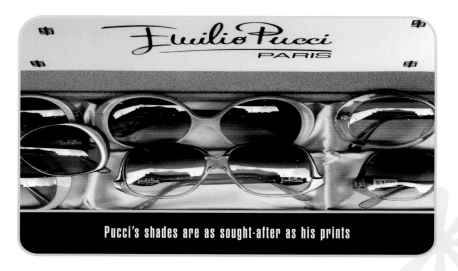

Pucci's shades are as sought-after as his prints

discover that all the big noises in twentieth-century fashion have also left a legacy of top-notch specs: Pucci, Cardin, Dior, YSL, Courrèges – all are here, along with a select group of more specialized names. Most fashionable of all is Cazal, a brand of glasses thrust into the spotlight in the early 1980s, when they became the ultimate style statement for rappers and hip-hop pioneers such as Grandmaster Flash. These were expensive, aspirational pieces even at the time, and today they fetch high prices from fans of their bold, confident, and quintessentially urban styling.

Prices average £150–400, and the styles are varied enough to suit every taste; there are understated, classic numbers alongside huge, technicolour frames by Pucci (which take some living up to). The Michael Caine look is always popular, so too is anything evoking Jackie O., and all frames can be fitted with prescription lenses as well as shades; there are even a few original Elton John numbers just for display. Above all, what impresses about C&G Vintage is not just its amazing stock, but its finger-on-the-pulse fashion sense, embracing everything from the catwalks to the latest street trends. Proof, if any more were needed, that a firm grip of the past is the hallmark of the cutting edge.

MAYFAIR

Gray's Antique Centre is a major destination for lovers of period fashion, and those with a taste for costume jewellery, compacts and delectable vintage bags should head for the ground floor HQ of Linda Bee. With more than 25 years in the business, Linda boasts a depth of knowledge that gives her a special place in

Linda Bee

Address: Stand L18-21, The Mews, Gray's Antique Market, 58 Davies St, W1
Hours: Mon–Fri 13:00–18:00
Telephone: 020 7629 5921 / 07956 276384
Tube: Bond St
Bus: 8

London's fashion community, as does her taste for the exotic, the beautiful and the whimsical from late Victoriana to the present day.

Deco features strongly, especially in the sizeable collection of perfume bottles, many with their contents intact. The bags meanwhile range from pre-war clutch numbers with beads and sequins, to rigid designs from the 1950s and 1960s; these include some real surprises, such as the amazing 1950s 'Beehive' bag in cream and caramel plastics, shaped like its namesake (and very exclusive even when it was made). Others feature fun designs, with cartoon poodles or bunches of cherries, while variations on the classic crocodile theme add a little understated chic.

Smaller accessories include a variety of compacts, all in tip-top condition and usually boasting some eye-catching decoration, such as the lovely example from the 1930s with drawings of sporty young things in their flannels and tennis skirts. The space is not huge, but everything is expertly chosen, and the standout items come and go in a flash. Film and television companies are regulars, and compete for the more unusual items with the remainder of Linda's ultra-discerning fan club.

One-time owner of Kensington Market and Antiquarius, and the genius behind Alfie's, Benny Gray has had an enormous impact on London's antiques trade. In recent years this has increasingly encompassed vintage clothing, and Gray's Antique Centre near Bond Street has already hit the headlines with the opening of Vintage Modes. Now, every May and September the venue also hosts the swanky, sophisticated yet entirely welcoming fashion event that is Vintage Mayfair. The show brings together several dozen of the country's leading dealers, presenting customers with a superb choice of clothing as well as saving them some serious mileage into the bargain. Younger, less established

Vintage Mayfair

Address: The Music Room, Gray's Antique Market, 26 South Molton Lane, W1
Hours: May & September, one Sunday from 12:00–18:00
Telephone: 020 7629 7034 (organizer Kirsty)
Web: www.vintagemodes.co.uk
Tube: Bond St
Bus: 8

Who needs Bond St. when there's Vintage Mayfair!

sellers are included, along with more experienced hands, and risk-taking is positively encouraged. Most surprising of all, given the location and the quality, are the very affordable prices.

Among the regulars are Mark and Cleo from C20 Vintage Fashions. Based in Exeter, theirs is a truly world-class concern boasting a museum-quality collection of classics, and a particular soft spot for home-grown talent (they supplied items for the Ossie Clarke exhibition at the V&A). Their range is enormous, from deco embroidery and 1930s bias-cut satin to chiffon tea gowns, 1960s chic and 1970s street-wear. In addition, they own a huge fashion archive for the use of designers and film companies. Other out-of-towners include Decades from Blackburn, Covet from Birmingham and Julia Gray from Bath.

Costume jewellery is plentiful, with a strong line-up of deco delectables from Kay du Bery and Helen Jones. Meanwhile Sonia B brings together a rich mix of distinctive items, ranging from Edwardian lace shirts to psychedelic dresses, along with beautiful textiles and silk scarves. And for handbag collectors, Hilary Proctor and Philippa Bowes offer a huge selection from the nineteenth century to the 1960s in designs for every occasion, including many with cameo-, turquoise-, or pearl-enriched clasps.

The Music Room, where the fair takes palace, enjoys good natural light and is spacious enough to allow dealers to be creative with their displays. Equally imaginative are the customers, who love to mix and match and put together a look they can call their own – individual, stylish, and not afraid to stand out from the crowd: in fact, very like Vintage Mayfair.

S ince opening in April 2003, Vintage Modes has become a major landmark on London's vintage clothing map. A large part of the basement at Gray's Market has been transformed into a stunning subterranean boudoir, complete with gilt, chandeliers and enough red plush to furnish an opera house. Grouped seamlessly in this space are seven separate dealers, whose wares make good the collective claim to

Vintage Modes

Address: The Mews, Gray's Antique Market, 58 Davies St, W1
Hours: Mon–Fri 10:00-18:00
Telephone: 020 7629 7034
Web: www.vintagemodes.co.uk
Tube: Bond St
Bus: 8

be 'a treasure house of vintage fashion'. The clothes themselves are beautifully displayed, with arrays of hats in backlit cabinets, forests of accessories on vintage stands, spectacular bridal arrangements, and rail upon rail of superior finery. There's also a central chill-out zone with comfy seating, a fountain, and enough space to test-drive your irresistible soon-to-be-purchases.

Each of the dealers brings something different to the mix, which as a result is rich, versatile and vibrant. On my last visit there was Biba and Balenciaga, Dior, Mary Quant, Ossie Clarke and ever-popular Pucci, to name but a few. Catwalk trends are followed very closely, whether it's the all-in-black Jean Muir look, a sudden craze for summer lawn dresses, or the so-far longer-lasting passion for all things 1950s and 1960s. Customers continue to favour styles that look emphatically of their time, and at Vintage Modes this could be anything from late Victorian to the 1980s.

Budget-wise, expect to pay a sensible price for unique and eminently wearable items that are guaranteed to be much loved; this could be from tens of pounds, to hundreds for major accessories and wardrobe basics, rising to occasional four-figure tickets for couture gems (and the little number 'attributed to Fortuny'!). With high-fashion honey-pots such as Bond St and South Molton St just around the corner, Vintage Modes is fast becoming a West End shopping institution. Look out, too, for the 'Vintage Mayfair' fashion fairs at the same address.

OXFORD STREET

John Lewis has always been a by-word for dependability, but that's never stopped them from occasionally dishing up a surprise or two. Most unexpected of all was the decision about six years ago to make space in the prime Oxford Street jewellery department for some sparklies of the vintage costume variety. But any doubts at the time have long since been dispelled, as the venture has proved to be a roaring success and the store now enjoys an enviable reputation in the world of high fashion.

John Lewis

Address: 300 Oxford St, W1
Hours: Mon-Sat 09:30-19:00 (till 20:00 on Thurs), Sun 12:00-18:00
Telephone: 020 7629 7711
Web: www.johnlewis.com
Tube: Oxford Circus
Bus: 7, 10, 25, 55, 176, 390

The secret behind this new-found fame is buyer Jacqueline Ebelthite, who not only conjures up an inexhaustible supply of goodies from the 1920s to the 1950s, but also supplies her own priceless expertise. Her parish is an island of display

Quality jewellery, honestly priced

cases very near the main entrance, and the items on show are only a fraction of the larger stock tucked away in drawers and cabinets. Brooches shaped like butterflies, bouquets and bees nestle among necklaces, earrings, bracelets and a selection of bags from the beaded to the clear lucite. There are vibrant, tropical colours, subdued pastels, enamels, and even a smattering of diamanté, all arranged with Jacqueline's trademark wit and eye for the extraordinary. Her reluctance to 'play safe' is one of the things that draws aficionados from far and wide, especially on a Thursday morning when she makes her weekly personal appearance.

Designers, milliners and theatre companies all make a regular pilgrimage, whilst collectors come for pieces by all the big names – Trifari, Napier, Lisner – pieces that are often snapped up within hours. But with around 100 new items added each week, there is always something for every taste. Newcomers are seduced by the gorgeous designs and by the reassuring 'wrapping' of the JL name, which often encourages them to make that all-important first vintage purchase. The effect is especially pronounced at Christmas, when stunning pieces put aside throughout the year are all brought together for a jaw-dropping display that never fails to create a stir.

For Jacqueline, as for her customers, one of the most exciting things about vintage costume jewellery is the ease with which it can be worn today. A 1950s brooch originally intended for a formal evening ensemble can look just as fabulous these days pinned to a denim jacket. And given the recent high street fascination with vintage clothing styles, a whole new generation has been discovering the fun of adding the perfect finishing touch to a modern dress or suitably tailored top. Prices average £30–50 for earrings, bracelets or brooches, whilst a matching set will cost around £100 (more for one of the Christmas specials!). Prices like these make a little fun and experimentation irresistible – especially when it's a great investment, too.

H ats off to Top Shop for putting vintage at the very centre of London's fashion map – in their flagship Oxford Street store. This is no mere bandwagoning either, but a commitment that goes back many years and continues to develop. Best of all, the clothes themselves are high quality, and fairly priced, too.

The womenswear takes up part of a basement floor, and on last viewing was placed right in front of a 'down' escalator for maximum effect. Signs and slogans making much use of the word 'vintage' cleverly mark out the space from the rest of the shop: in fact, the layout of the whole floor has recently won awards, and is always being revamped to keep the presentation fresh. Tiered podiums topped with shoes and bags make a colourful display in summer months when 1980s two-tones mix it with 1960s pastels. The full range of footwear is lined up on shelves further back – with lots more killer heels and dinky details – whilst other accessories such as belts and scarves spill over on to a separate area of their own.

But the main attraction is the day- and eveningwear, which comes in an enormous range of styles from the 1950s to the 1980s. Each decade makes a good showing, with the earliest yielding some exquisite cocktail

Top Shop

Address: 214 Oxford St, W1
Hours: Mon–Sat 09:00–20:00 (till 21:00 on Thurs), Sun 11:00–17:00
Telephone: 020 7927 7634
Web: www.topshop.co.uk
Tube: Oxford Circus
Bus: 3, 7, 8, 10, 25, 55, 73, 98, 176, 390

Vintage comes to Oxford Street

and party dresses. Expect to find elegant, Givenchyesque numbers as well as elaborate confections in chiffon and organza, all in excellent condition. Also from the glamour era are some natty tailored jackets that segue nicely into a stash of wide-lapelled 1970s versions. Nineteen-sixties separates and chic cotton dresses also mingle on the rails with T-shirts, kilts and halter-neck tops.

Given the location, the most surprising news is that very little here costs more than £70. This not only mirrors Top Shop's keen pricing on contemporary fashions, but also appeals to younger customers on limited budgets, who have been snapping up the vintage stuff as much for fun everyday wear as for special occasions.

The whole set-up revolves around a carefully managed portfolio of expert suppliers, each of whom brings something different to the party; these include 'Style Generation' for shoes, 'Jeepers Creepers' for sunglasses, and 'Peekaboo' for bags and general clothing. 'Vintage Princess' supplies most of the more glamorous dresses that have proved a huge hit, whilst the mainstay of the stock has for some years been the Vintage Clothing Company (that also owns Pop Boutique in Monmouth Street). Up on the first floor the same formula also underpins a growing selection of menswear, where the flight bags, 1970s leather jackets and casual shirts are all proving popular. So too – to general surprise – are some rather more daring jumpsuits!

SOHO

A s Soho yields up ever more space to glitzy new bars and coffee shops, a spot such as Walker's Court should be subject to a conservation order, preserving as it does an old-school air of sleaze and sin all wrapped up in a dodgy little alleyway. Somehow it seems only right that in among the neon and the stocking tops there should also be a sign for a tattoo parlour, even if 'body art' is now so mainstream that it can be had at Selfridge's.

Diamond Jacks

Address: 5 Walker's Court, Soho, W1
Hours: Mon–Sat 11:00––18:00, Sun 12:00–17:00
Telephone: 020 7437 0605
Web: www.diamondjacks.co.uk
Tube: Piccadilly Circus
Bus: 14, 19, 38

A narrow staircase leads up from the street and opens out into a pleasant waiting room hung with colourful designs; through a glass partition can be seen owner Ian Kaye, hard at work with his needles. This parlour boasts quite a history, having once been home to the legendary Dennis Cockell. Dennis made a huge contribution to the UK scene in terms of original artwork and personal style, and in his time inked the likes of 'The Stray Cats', Steve Jones from the 'Pistols' and many more. He's moved on now, but a wide range of Cockell designs are still included in Ian's portfolio, along with Sailor Jerry classics, wicked Vince Ray 'toons, and a host of traditional pin-ups, hearts, roses and dice.

The retro stuff is most popular with the younger European crowd, who make a point of dropping by whilst they're in London. Locals, it seems, are still in thrall to tribal and Celtic motifs. A Cockell original measuring four by five inches, using traditional flat colours (and lots of greens and reds), will take an hour or so to complete and cost around £70. Custom work and pin-striping can be arranged, but these work out more expensive. Best of all, come and have a browse through what's on the walls, and Ian will gladly talk things through. Hepcats, rockers and lounge lizards especially welcome!

50s Hula Girl tattoo, as drawn by Dennis Cockell

For more than forty years the northern end of Soho's Berwick Street has been brightened by the premises of unique stylist and tailor-to-the-stars, Eddie Kerr. Over that time his windows have displayed a peerless succession of sharp suits, fine cloths and sometimes outrageous jackets, which have marked this out as something rather different from your average gentlemen's clothier.

Now joined by son Chris, 'Mr Eddie' is first and foremost a top quality bespoke tailor. Traditional two- and three-piece suits are his stock-in-trade, along with eveningwear, jackets and trousers. But this is also a great place to come for authentically 1960s- or 1970s-styled, made-to-measure clothing, not least because Mr Eddie was there the first time round and is a stickler for period detail. In days gone by, Teddy Boys and Mods came here in droves, and though their numbers are far fewer now, all the appropriate styles can still be had for the asking.

Mr Eddie's kept busier these days by an enviable list of stage and screen personalities who look to him to conjure up flamboyant costumes, many of which have a cool, retro look. Notable examples include coats for Ewan McGregor, Vic Reeves' suits for *Randall & Hopkirk*, and just about all of Graham Norton's jackets.

Eddie Kerr

Address: 52 Berwick St, W1
Hours: Mon–Fri 08:00–17:30, Sat 08:30–13:00
Telephone: 020 7437 3727
Web: www.eddiekerr.co.uk
Tube: Oxford Circus
Bus: 7, 8, 10, 25, 55, 73, 98, 176, 390

Tailoring by the master, Eddie Kerr

Film and television companies also commission a huge range of gentlemen's clothes for productions that could be set in any period of time, from the Victorian era onwards. The most unusual job without a doubt was for PG Tips, who once decided that their famous chimps should be kitted out in bespoke pin-striped suits.

For suits of a more typical size, prices average £850, whilst trousers are more like £75, and the process takes around three weeks from first measurements to delivery (depending on the availability of customers for refitting). Styles go in and out of fashion, and Eddie's own personal fave is probably the slim-fit 1970s body shape that is now in vogue again, albeit minus the full-scale lapels of the originals.

One thing's for sure, as institutions go, they don't come much more approachable than this.

E very few years the high street stores rediscover the 1960s: the rails suddenly become full of geometric prints and mini dresses, and the newspapers once again dust off their headlines about the latest 'Mod revival'. All of which is fine if you're happy with the general look, but bone fide Modernists have always taken their clothing very seriously; and as far as they're concerned, that means top-notch tailoring.

Tailoring 2000

Address: 51 Lexington St, W1
Hours: Phone first
Telephone: 020 7439 1633 /
07960 943231
Tube: Oxford Circus/Piccadilly Circus
Bus: 3, 6, 12, 13, 15, 23, 88, 94, 139, 159, 453

For more than 25 years true believers have been coming to Chris in his first floor Soho workshop (and before that they came to see his uncle!). He's a legend among 1960s enthusiasts the world over, especially in Europe, where many a German, Swiss or French 'face' would look a lot less authentically dapper were it not for the work of Tailoring 2000.

Suits, skirts, shirts, trousers, waistcoats and dresses can all be made to the most exacting requirements. Once he's measured you up, there's almost nothing Chris won't put his needle to (he says he'll make 'everything but aeroplanes'). Customers regularly confront him with grainy images from old magazines, or stills from films, showing the styles they'd like him to copy. Classic hipsters are always popular, and will set you back around £90. These might have extra-wide belt loops, with big circular cut-outs to display the belt passing through, or the trousers might be in bright green with loops in contrasting purple. Chris's customers really appreciate his close attention to detail, as this is just the sort of thing that marks out the bespoke gear from the mass-produced variety.

A dress typically works out at about £250, whilst a superb suit will dent your bank balance by upwards of £650 (not including materials). The cloths used are exclusive to Tailoring 2000, and some are designed in-house. All the work is done on the premises, where there's even a machine for turning out fabric-covered buttons (a rare 1960s touch that will set off any outfit to a tee). Making-up time is usually around three to four weeks, depending on the time of year.

Outside the Mod scene customers include film and television companies, as well as connoisseurs of other 1960s music-based styles, notably ska. Chris's son, George, is poised to take over the business in the near future and carry on the grand family tradition. I wouldn't mind betting some of the longer-term customers are likewise even now packing off their sons and daughters to Lexington Street to be kitted out with some decent clobber.

VICTORIA

Some names say it all. This long-established store is summed up perfectly by an image of overflowing and inexhaustible supply – and indeed, to explore the stock thoroughly would take at least a week. Fortunately, owner Jerry and colleague Ralph know exactly where everything is, so if you arrive with a view to picking up a 1950s cocktail dress, or a 1960s belted jacket, they'll point you in the right direction.

Cornucopia

Address: 12 Upper Tachbrook Street, SW1
Hours: Daily 11:00–18:00
Telephone: 020 7828 5752
Tube/rail: Victoria
Bus: 2, 36, 185, 436

Items date from the 1920s to the 1970s, and prices average around £25. Shoes are a speciality, with tiered shelves of them taking up much of one wall. Most of the footwear is from the 1940s or 1950s, and includes fluffy mules as well as sensible daywear, strappy slingbacks and classic kitten heels. Earlier pairs from as far back as the 1920s do also turn up, but as is the case with all such older clothing, it certainly helps if you're on the small side.

Cornucopia is also very strong on full-length gowns and eveningwear, with clubbable locals often dropping by to pick up something that little bit different for a party or a ball. Floor-standing rails support a multitude of jackets and blouses,

'So many clothes, so little time.'
Customers are spoilt for choice at Cornucopia

whilst up above them – in a great canopy of multicoloured fabrics – hang the skirts of a hundred printed-cotton frocks, peignoirs, and satin shifts. Just behind the window display is even a selection of bridalwear. Meanwhile, brightening up the walls are velvet capes, embroidered shawls and beaded dresses, which at £200—300 mark out the upper limit for prices. A large collection of costume jewellery lurks in the cabinets by the counter, and if you still have any strength there's also a marvellous stock of hats, which will keep you busy for hours. A must-see: but get in training first!

For 50 years, bands have been buying their gear from Charing Cross Road and London's very own Tin Pan Alley (aka Denmark Street). For almost as long, musical inspiration has been supplied by the record shops of nearby Hanway Street.

TOTTENHAM COURT ROAD

In a street of shops jam-packed with vintage musical gear, pride of place must surely go to the world-renowned insitution that is Andy's Guitars. The store itself is as much a part of rock history as are the covetable items it sells.

Starting out as a basement repair service in 1978, the business now spans five floors and includes among its staff no fewer than four fully qualified 'luthiers', who can custom-build an instrument from scratch. The front-of-house team is no less impressive: ask one of them for a quick demo, and you might be obliged by Tim, who for 20 years toured with rock gods Led Zep. As a master technician he's still very much in demand, and if he's not in the shop it's usually because he's out on the road with some young hopeful like Ray Davies. Look out, too, for colleague Dave, who started out with Gene Vincent and the Everlys.

For all its impeccable rock pedigree, Andy's remains as friendly a place as you could hope for. Customers receive the same care and attention whatever their budget, and a 'starter pack' of guitar, amp, strap and leads can be had for as little as £200. But the undeniable stars of the show are the vintage numbers. A 1902 Washburn in Brazilian rosewood is about as early as they come, though at around £4000 is far from the priciest. The big money is reserved for the classic designs from the 1950s, when Fender and Gibson burst on to the scene and gave the

Andy's Guitars Andy's Drums

Address: 27 Denmark St, WC2
Hours: Mon–Fri 10:00–20:00,
Sat 12:30–18:30
Telephone: 020 7836 4522 (Drums)
/ 020 7916 5080 (Guitars)
Web: www.andysguitarnet.com
Tube: Tottenham Court Rd
Bus: 14, 19, 24, 29, 38, 176

Follow in the footsteps of Jimmy Page and finger some frets at world-renowned Andy's Guitars

world the templates which to this day still define the look, feel and sound of an electric guitar.

Recent gems in stock include a 1952 Telecaster, one of the first of its kind, a 1958 Jazzmaster, and an all-original 1959 Gibson '335' – for a plectrum-wilting £15,000. Then again, you'll need at least that to get your hands on a pristine early Stratocaster. But if it's the look that counts, then a dinky 'Danelectro' will cost around £1000 and look every inch a product of the 'Swinging Sixties'. Andy's also has a great selection of vintage amps, so you can hear these beasts the way they're meant to be heard – amplified by some hot, fat valves courtesy of Vox or Selmer.

Over the years, customers have included a whole pantheon of the guitar world's great and good, from Jimmy Page and Rory Gallagher to groups such as Blur, Oasis, the Red Hot Chili Peppers and too many more to mention. Musical styles may come and go, but when it comes to the instruments themselves, each new generation eventually finds its own way back to those post-war classics that helped put rock'n'roll on the map.

Tucked away behind Andy's Guitars is the sister shop, Andy's Drums, doing for 'skins' what the other does for strings. When he launched the business in 2003, owner Tom filled the shelves with his own prized collection of vintage drums. Since then he's built an enviable reputation as one of the select few to stock the kits that put the backbeat into the golden age of pop.

Items sometimes date from as far back as the 1920s, but most are from the 1940s to the 1970s. Ludwig remains the biggest seller, for ever earmarked as 'The Beatles' brand of choice, and a set of 'Black Beauties', or one in gorgeous 'champagne sparkle', is guaranteed to add a special razzmatazz to any new-fangled beat combo. Recent years have also seen a huge increase in demand for early 1970s styles in transparent 'Vistalite' (especially in amber). A five-piece kit, including snare, will set you back around £1300. Ironically, UK buyers tend to prefer the US-made kits by Rogers or Gretsch, whilst US customers have a soft spot for British-manufactured designs. Perhaps the National Trust should step in and save for the nation all those lovely States-bound tom toms and 24in bass drums by Premier, Carlton, Edgware, Autocrat and Ajax!

Customers on both sides of the Atlantic include lifelong devotees of particular brands, as well as younger players who value not only the look, but also that special sound that only vintage equipment can provide. Tom is keen to point out the superb quality of workmanship on the older instruments, which will always give them the edge over modern copies. His kits are already doing sterling service for big-name acts such as Coldplay and the Manic Street Preachers, and the list is set to grow.

A record shop has stood on this site since the mid-1960s, when London's soul fans used to come in search of imports at the legendary 'Contempo'. As the later 'Vibe', it numbered Shane McGowan among its staff, and now it's called 'JBs', where I wouldn't mind betting some of those Contempo 45s still change hands from time to time.

Singles are a strong point, taking in everything from 1950s blues and rock'n'roll to soul, punk and funk. Prices start from a few pounds and can reach giddy, triple-figured heights for rarities such as Herman Griffin's *I Need You* (an early Berry Gordy production). The choice of LPs is equally wide, and includes a mixture of originals and fairly priced reissues. Among current gems, pride of place for out-and-out kookiness goes to the soundtrack of late 1960s surrealist flick *Viva La Muerte* (quite indescribable!). With space at a premium, vinyl is favoured over CDs, and the walls are pressed into service for displaying T-shirts of Brian Jones and other assorted icons.

As for trends, soul remains a perennial favourite, whilst other genres enjoy their ups and downs.

JBs

Address: 36 Hanway St, W1
Hours: Mon–Sat 12:00–19:00
(plus Sundays in summer)
Telephone: 020 7436 4063
Tube: Tottenham Court Rd
Bus: 10, 73, 390

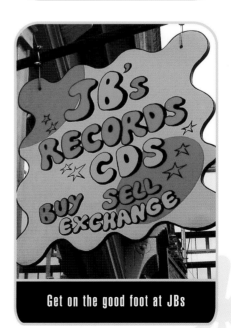

Get on the good foot at JBs

Currently in vogue with DJs and collectors alike is the post-punk, white-boy funk of bands such as 'A Certain Ratio' (fondly remembered not only for their music but for their splendid khaki shorts). But JBs isn't the kind of place where you feel you can only open your mouth if you're after something impossibly obscure: ask for anything at all and you'll get a sensible answer, if not the record itself. The shop also makes a major contribution to London's retro nightlife by supplying singles for the jukebox at neighbouring Bradley's Spanish Bar.

More than just a shop, Macari's is a much-loved landmark, family run since 1958 and boasting a history that puts it at the heart of Britain's post-war popular music boom. Back in the 1960s the company was one of the world's leading manufacturers of effects pedals, turning out truckloads of snazzy gizmos under the legendary 'Coloursound' name. Listening to the Yardbirds or early Led Zep, one can hear Macari's circuits hard at work, and though original 'Tone Benders' are now collectors' items, quality reproductions are among the many attractions at the store today.

The bulk of the space is given over to a world-class line-up of vintage guitars, along with a highly respected brass and wind section, too. Classic Fenders and Gibsons plaster the walls, along with enough examples from other illustrious marques to fill a museum: there are Epiphones, Rickenbackers, Guilds, Hofners, and of course a

Macari's

Address: 92–94 Charing Cross Rd, WC2
Hours: Mon-Sat 10:00-17:30
Telephone: 020 7836 2856
Web: www.macaris.co.uk
Tube: Tottenham Court Rd/Leicester Sq
Bus: 14, 19, 24, 29, 38, 176

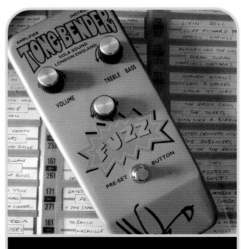

Caught by the fuzz at FX masters, Macari's

Gretsch or two to complete the set. Prices start at a few hundred pounds and rise to many thousands, whilst customers range from starry-eyed teenagers to life-long players and connoisseurs. The prize for the earliest six-string in the shop goes to the 1924 Gibson L4, as featured in the *Ultimate Guitar Book* and on sale for around £2000.

Most first-time vintage buyers come in search of something a little more familiar, such as the 1970s versions of classic 1950s designs. Then still US-made, and to a high standard, these offer the look of the originals and something of their magical sound, but for a fraction of the price. Perhaps enjoying most demand of late has been the Telecaster, buoyed up by the renaissance of the roughed-up Detroit sound. But a shift in taste could just as easily see the focus turn towards the Les Paul or iconic Strat.

Bands in search of inspiration could always ask to hear an original 1970s Stylophone (£60—£100), or even a totally loopy Theremin, invented in the 1920s but perhaps the perfect centrepiece for any psychedelic act. Owners Steve and Anthony keep some of the choicest items in their lair downstairs, including one of Jon Entwistle's basses, and the original sign from one-time neighbour, the legendary bookshop '84 Charing Cross Road'.

Ah, Hanway Street! So much more than a cut-through between Oxford Street and Tottenham Court Road. Much of it was bought up by two Spanish brothers in the 1950s, and legend has it that they owned the first espresso machine in London. Their restaurants still add Andalusian colour to the road's unique charm today. In the 1970s

On The Beat

Address: 22 Hanway St, W1
Hours: Mon–Sat 11:00–19:00
Telephone: 020 7637 8934
Tube: Tottenham Court Rd
Bus: 10, 73, 390

another star attraction was the cupboard-sized Daddy Kool, which drew dub addicts from far and wide. No vinyl-hunting trip was complete back then without also checking out the rarities at 'Luigi & The Boys', and the same still holds true today, only the shop is now called 'On The Beat'.

Funnily enough, the music from the late 1970s and early 1980s is currently enjoying something of a boom; younger customers especially are rediscovering the New Wave energy of bands such as Prag Vec or Gang of Four, on original picture-sleeved 45s. On The Beat's full range is enormous and spread over two rooms, with singles and CDs in the front, LPs and magazines at

The sounds the megastores don't reach

the back. There are also various photos of rock gods and pop icons, some of which are ex-promo material selling for a few pounds, whilst others are unpublished prints (usually of live shows) priced suicidally cheap at £20—£40. Albums average £10, but occasional rarities go for several hundred (as do some EPs).

The jam-packed racks allow just enough room for dividers that announce 'Female Vocal', 'Garage Punk' or even 'Australian/NZ Artists' (and that means Split Enz, not Kylie). On the walls, 1970s issues of *NME* or *Sounds* (£3) fight for space with vintage editions of *Rolling Stone* (£8), and books on everyone from Bowie to Badfinger.

Many's the time I've walked past Vintage and Rare, or rather *tried* to: somehow I always find myself lingering at the window, trying not to drool over the treasures inside. Since 1982 this shop has been tempting musos with the best in classic American guitars. The stock concentrates on iconic designs from the 1950s and 1960s, but extends well beyond the usual famous names to include a host of supporting acts. My eye was caught by a 1953 Guild 'Aristocrat' with hollow body and spruce top,

Vintage and Rare Guitars

Address: 6 Denmark St, WC2
Hours: Mon-Sat 10:00–18:00, Sun 12:00–16:00
Telephone: 020 7240 7500
www.vintageandrareguitars.com
Tube/rail: Tottenham Court Rd
Bus: 14, 19, 24, 29, 38, 176

exactly the kind once played by John Lee Hooker (and on sale for around £1500). Elsewhere there are Rickenbackers, Kays, Epiphones, Hofners and Harmonys, along with enough real obscurities to quicken any collector's pulse. Take the

'Guyatone', which could only have come from the 1950s, but less predictably turns out to have been made in Japan. Or the Czech-made Neoton 'Grazioso', a name hardly written large in the annals of guitar history, but all the same deserving a footnote as the young George Harrison's instrument of choice. Western Swing bands and born-again Delta bluesmen are also catered for, with a rare collection of lap steel, slide and tenor guitars, many of which can hold their own simply as objects of superb design.

Then of course there are the main turns that always draw a crowd: Fender, Gibson, and not forgetting Gretsch. I'm hardly alone in thinking there's something special about a big, bold, hollow-bodied Gretsch: from their sinuous sound-holes to their 'touch me' knobs and frets, they are the pin-ups of the musical world and the very embodiment of rock'n'roll. Not surprisingly the 1950s originals are hugely popular, and a 'White Falcon' or a 'Chet Atkins Country Gentleman' can easily cost £5,000. Likewise classic Gibsons, such as the 'SG' or 'Explorer', also fetch serious bucks – though it's worth remembering that a much more affordable Epiphone like the 'Broadway' (£2k) was made at the same factory, and to Gibson's same exacting standards, up until the mid-1960s.

'Vintage and Rare' is just as great a place to *talk* guitars, as buy them. Owner Adam was a roadie with The Clash and is now a one-man oral history of all things that twang. Customers come from all over the world, especially the US, where clued-up investors are proving ever more keen to buy back their heritage.

Perk up your plectrum at Vintage & Rare

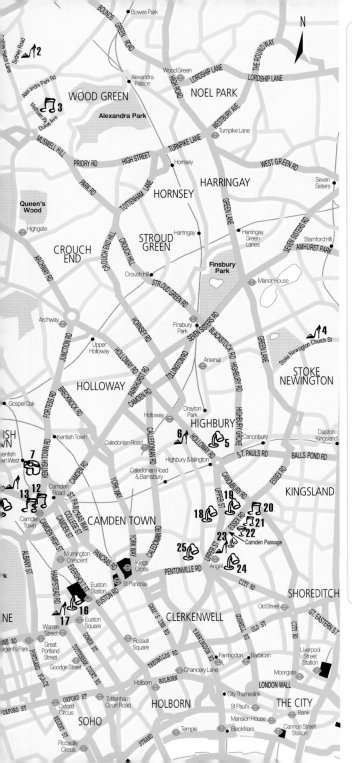

north

In the *Ace* and the *S&M* North London boasts two shining examples of classic cafes saved for the nation – and not a lottery grant in sight! Both preserve a vital link with Britain's social past, whilst dishing up a killer breakfast.

ISLINGTON

M any will remember Alfredo's, the Islington institution that was immortalized in Quadrophenia and for 80 years the very model of a family-owned, Italian-run, but also quintessentially British caff, welcoming locals and visitors alike. Like great country estates – and no less a part of our cultural heritage – London's classic cafés are always in need of a new generation to keep them alive

The S&M Café (formerly Alfredo's)

Address: 4–6 Essex Rd, N1
Hours: Mon–Fri 08:00–2:30, Sat 09:00–24:00, Sun 09:00–22:30
Telephone: 020 7359 5361
Tube/rail: Angel/Essex Rd
Bus: 38, 56 73, 341, 476

although all too often this doesn't come to pass. For a while it looked as if Alfredo's future hung in the balance, until along came Kevin Finch – restaurateur, design-devotee and canny businessman – who took over the site and saved it for the nation. Alfredo's was duly reborn in 2003 as the 'Sausage and Mash Café'.

There are other S&M Cafés in what is now a small chain (including one under Notting Hill's Westway), but none of them is quite like this. With an extraordinary attention to detail, the original interior has been painstakingly restored. The project took a whole year and the biggest challenge was finding the right materials. Whilst a whole industry has grown up to help revive a Tudor barn or a Cotswold cottage, try replacing some 50-year old formica, and you're on your own. Or take humble lino: authentically post-war styles in solid, non-flecked colours are about as common today as a ten-shilling note! It's no wonder that since taking on Alfredo's, Kevin has evolved from a mere fan of classic materials into a *bona fide* expert.

It's OK, they take 'new money' too! The legendary Alfredo's lives on as The S&M Café

As for the food, today's menu retains many old favourites, including home-made soups, boiled egg and soldiers, and the obligatory bacon sarnie. But the pièce de resistance is, of course, the sausage and mash, which comes in a huge variety of guises. The humble banger of old is now joined by such gourmet delights as 'pork, stilton and celery', or even sausages made from 'chicken, asparagus and parmesan cheese'! All can be topped with a selection of mouth-watering gravies (wild mushroom, wholegrain mustard with chilli) and bedded down in great heaps of mash, from regular to the bubble-and-squeak special. Vegetarians are catered for, too, with no fewer than four meat-free options among the dozen-strong sausage line-up. For those who still have the room, puds offer a comforting return to tradition with fruit crumble and Bird's custard high on the agenda.

Given that Alfredo's was for so long a vital part of the local community, Kevin was adamant that things shouldn't change, and his success is borne out by the diverse crowd of diners from families and friends to couples, business types and single people young and old. In its perfect marriage of past and present, the S&M Café is a rare example of what modernization should be. And it even does takeaway!

STONEBRIDGE

At the Royal Observatory in Greenwich is a metal strip on the ground that marks the exact line of the meridian. The true centre of the world, however, lies a few miles north in Stonebridge Park, at the one and only Ace Café.

Erected in 1938, this deco-inspired building seemed to have reached the end of a short but illustrious life when in 1969 it closed its doors. But its importance was never forgotten by the legions of British Bike enthusiasts, for whom it had been a spiritual home

The Ace Café

Address: Ace Corner, Old North Circular Rd (junction with Beresford Avenue), Stonebridge, NW10
Hours: Weekdays 07:00-23:00, weekends 07:00-late
Telephone: 020 8961 1000
Web: www.ace-cafe-london.com
Tube/rail: Stonebridge Park
Bus: 112, 224

back in the days when the UK led the world in two-wheeled engineering. The scale of their affection and respect became clear in 1994, on the 25th anniversary of the café's closure, when a reunion on the site brought together no fewer than 12,000 devotees; this turnout served to confirm in the mind of organizer Mark

Wilsmore that his dream of reopening the old place might one day come true.

An ex-cop with a lifetime's love of bikes and rock'n'roll, Mark had already begun to muster support, and further reunions throughout the nineties culminated in the purchase of a part of the freehold in 1997. 'Ace Corner' opened for business soon after, but not until the departure of the resident tyre company did the whole building finally become vacant, and in 2001 the Ace Café was at last reopened.

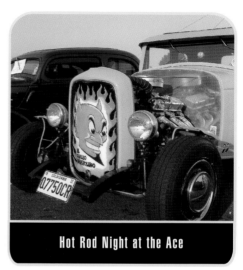

Hot Rod Night at the Ace

The café today offers something for everybody, with all-day fry-ups, decent coffee, a great bar, and regular live music to fire up the night-time get-togethers for every kind of vehicle from scooters to Hot Rods. As home to the ''59 Club' – the largest motorcycle club in the world – bikes still take centre stage at the Ace, especially on Sundays, but Mark is keen to promote the venue as a meeting place for 'petrol heads' of every persuasion, which in practice means just about 'anything except lawnmowers'. The reborn café has been equally successful in attracting a music-loving crowd who come to hear authentic rock'n'roll in an ideal setting. With a bar open nightly and a late licence at weekends, the only reason ever to go home is for an occasional change of clothes.

As much as Mark is excited by the future of the Ace, he's also intensely aware of its past. By restoring the café to life he's re-established a link with its history and with all the things it has meant for generations of bikers and rock'n'rollers alike. Gene Vincent came here, as did The Beatles, and to come to the Ace today is to follow in the footsteps of all the speed-crazed, hopped-up Big Beat fanatics, famous and unsung, glorious and desperate, who have ever passed between these walls in search of tea, chips, a pint or a spark plug. Above all, the Ace is a unique celebration of Britishness, something that politicians and bureaucrats seem to find hard to define, but which the rest of us know in our bones. The only mystery is why Mark hasn't yet received a knighthood. Perhaps someone should organize a rally!

Islington and Camden offer an enormous range of design originals from modernist masterpieces to playful pop. North London is also home to a tuneful trio of specialists in wind-up gramophones, vintage radios and fabulous 50s jukeboxes.

CHALK FARM

Boom! is a bombshell of a shop, with probably the best displayed stock of mid-century furniture and design anywhere in London. Having made the move from Chalk Farm, the space in Primrose Hill is now so vast as to allow great vistas of Scandinavian sideboards and Italian lighting. One of the best visual effects is on entering the shop, where a short internal flight of stairs leads

Boom! Interiors

Address: 115-117 Regent's Park Rd, Primrose Hill, NW1
Hours: Mon-Sat 12:00-18:00
Telephone: 020 7722 6622
Web: www.boominteriors.com
Tube/rail: Chalk Farm
Bus: 31

to a raised ground floor. As a result, one's first view of the main room is from an unusual carpet-level angle, which nicely frames everything from the rugs to the chandeliers. Other rooms open off in every direction, and each one is not so much stocked as fully furnished – a sitting room here, a bedroom there, with sympathetic items so artfully arranged that one half expects to find someone at home. (It comes as no surprise to learn that owner Phil Cowan is a much sought-after interior designer.) Presentation is further enhanced by informative labels on the items themselves, which are mostly 1950s to 1970s with occasional modern extras – such as bedding – to help complete the room layouts.

Much of the furniture is of the wooden, craftsman-built variety, which means the Danes make a good showing. But so too do the Brits, with cabinets by John and Sylvia Reid, sofas by Gordon Russell, and some glamorous late 1960s pieces by Merrow Associates. In fact, one of Phil's current favourites is an attractive little oak table made in 1956 by the UK company 'Stag'. Its modernist, almost

Italian lights and Scandinavian sideboards fill just one of the stunning design-scapes at 'Boom! Interiors'

'Bauhaus' feel epitomizes the way in which British designers at that time looked to pre-war ideals for the perfect expression of our post-war austerity.

For those on a limited budget the best bet is to check out the lighting, which starts at under £100 (and rises to £2000–£3000). An entry-level sideboard is around £800, whilst a stunner will set you back more like £4500. Top prices are reserved for the art, which is strong on Op and Pop. A massive spread of Lichtenstein's 'Wallpaper' really pushes the boat out at £12,000, though there are always much more affordable prints from house artist Vasarely. Boom! is all about selling top quality items that will look as good in 50 years time as they do today – and right now they look amazing!

Pick up *The History of Chairs*, or any of those big fat books on twentieth-century design, and in among the graceful forms by Eames and Aalto you'll also find some truly radical items that test to the limit the marriage of form and function. They leap off the page, but outside a museum you never expect to encounter them in the flesh — unless, that is, you're a regular at CO2, which wins the prize for the most memorable item of furniture I've yet come across in a shop. Paolo Ruffi's

CO2 Modern Designs

Address: Ground Floor, The Horse Hospital, Stables Market, Chalk Farm Rd, Camden, NW1
Hours: Sat & Sun 10:00—18:00
Telephone: 020 7609 0857 / 07957 278043
Tube/rail: Chalk Farm/Camden Town
Bus: 24, 27, 31, 168

1973-designed 'Nest' is exactly that: a giant bird's nest with strips of foam for twigs and three egg-shaped cushions to complete the effect. As sofas go, it's a bit out of the ordinary, and as prices go, so is £12,000; but bear in mind that you're unlikely ever to see one again (the question is: would you *want* to?).

Owners Claudio and Patrick have an eye for the bold or unusual, especially when it comes to the brightly coloured, synthetic world of Pop. On entering the shop's vaulted space one's eye might be caught by Verner Panton's wall-mounted screens – huge arrangements of interlocking hemispheres in red and blue plastic – or perhaps by a pair of silver-sided armchairs designed by Pierre Cardin. Meanwhile Aarnio's 'Tomato' chair, consisting of three conjoined globes, looks at first like an alien life form taking a nap (1971, £1200). But there are also less futuristic designs that in their own understated way, equally command our attention: for example, the

Eames 1950 'Bikini' rocker chair (so called for its two triangles of fabric, joined by a thread), or the Saturno sofa, designed by Rinaldi in 1957 but so forward looking that at first it appears to be no older than the 1980s (very rare too, hence the £2400 price tag).

For those with a limited budget there are late 1960s Joe Colombo chairs for under £100. These come in black or white moulded plastic, and were featured time and again in UK design books up until the early 1970s. The more expensive items naturally attract a more established type of buyer, but CO2 is the sort of shop that in the course of any weekend will see hundreds of younger visitors relishing its space-age designs (on their way round the market). My guess is that, a few years from now, some of them will be back in search of their very own bird's nest.

Space-age hi-fi from Philips

Whilst there has never been more interest in mid-century design, London has surprisingly few specialists in 1950s Americana. All the more reason to make a bee-line for 'Out Of Time', which takes regular shipments from the States of all manner of items from the rock'n'roll era. Owner Chris Farlowe is better known for an

Out of Time

Address: 1st Floor, The Horse Hospital, Stables Market, Chalk Farm Rd, NW1
Hours: Sat & Sun 10:00-18:00
Tube/rail: Chalk Farm/Camden Town
Bus: 24, 27, 31, 168

earlier *Out Of Time*, namely the song he took to Number 1 in the charts in 1966. These days, with assistants Bill and Trevor, he has a regular gig at the Stables Market, where the stock can usually be counted on to include at least one diner-style kitchen table with classic chrome frame and pink- or blue-spangled surface. Add three or four matching dining chairs into the bargain, and these beauties

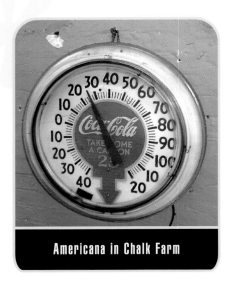

Americana in Chalk Farm

typically sell for around £500.

Characterful one-offs could be almost anything from a giant wheel-sized shop thermometer advertizing Coke (very collectable), to a stylish corner cocktail cabinet. My own recent favourite was the stunning 'Jet Pilot' bicycle made in 1959; with its graceful curves, fighter-plane motifs and fully working electric horn and lights, it's a case of 'hold the Maserati, I'll take one of *these*!'. Also on offer is a range of home-grown retro items such as 'English Electric' fridges, clocks and lamps. The stock turns over fast – especially the larger items – so remember to pop back.

S ince moving from Alfie's four years ago, owner Anna has made the most of the increased elbow room at the Stables Market, particularly when it comes to stocking larger items. These might include a pair of 1970s leather sofas made by Poltronova, and arranged with sympathetic cabinets and lamps as if in some chic,

Sambataro

Address: Unit 85, opp. The Horse Hospital, Stables Market, Chalk Farm Rd, NW1
Hours: Fri-Sun 10:00-18:00
Telephone: 07813 842188
Tube/rail: Chalk Farm/Camden Town
Bus: 24, 27, 31, 168

Milanese sitting room. But the most sizeable pieces of all – and the most unusual – are the spectacular home-use bars. Unlike the free-standing cocktail units of the 1950s, which are not much bigger than a chest of drawers, these 1960s Italian versions combine a counter with a separate head-height display module, the two set apart but joined by a common plinth. These one-piece wonders would add instant sophistication to any residential space, from a family dining room to a swish bachelor pad. Prices start from as little as £650, rising to more like £2400 for something in rosewood veneer with chromed edging and black leather upholstery. Pull up a stool and I'm sure a Martini never tasted better!

Items are mainly from the 1940s to the 1970s, with occasional forays back into the pre-war era, when Italy in fact produced some of its most forward-looking creations. Anna enthuses over Pietro Chiesa's all-glass table from 1934, made from one continuous sheet and still looking utterly contemporary today. Among current stock, her favourites include a pair of the same designer's simple but classic ceiling lights from 1933 (£850 each). All the pieces here are chosen not only for their design quality, but also for their condition, which is generally very high with minimal restoration.

Many a Camden dealer might have joked 'my other shop's in Rome', but in Sergio Guazzelli's case, it's true. His space in the Horse Hospital accommodates perhaps one tenth of his total stock, though as a taster it works admirably. The items map out major design trends in furniture and lighting from the 1920s to the 1980s, and their high quality is evident at once.

Among the earlier pieces are French Deco chairs in walnut and 'bird's eye' maple (so called for the effect in the grain, and a real period favourite); these make a perfect match with English 1930s standard lamps complete with wooden shades. Bringing us more up to date is a good selection of Italian chandeliers and wall lights, including gems by Magistretti, and handsome 1960s desks in Danish

Sergio Guazzelli

Address: Ground Floor, The Horse Hospital, Stables Market, Chalk Farm Rd, NW1
Hours: Sat & Sun 10:00—18:00
Telephone: 07956 645492
Tube/rail: Chalk Farm/Camden Town
Bus: 24, 27, 31, 168

Magistretti ceiling light

rosewood. You might have seen some of Sergio's wares if you've ever visited Mother Bar in Old Street; otherwise, ask to take a look at his photo album to get a feel for the full range on offer.

EDGWARE ROAD

S pare a thought for the humble poster: pasted up, then torn down — it has a short and precarious life. But every so often one or two escape the cull, and so it is that we can still enjoy the stunning works of graphic design you'll find at this unique outlet in Alfie's Antique Centre.

Liz Farrow has been collecting posters since she was a teenager, and dealing in them since 1960 – so she sure knows her stuff! Subjects cover 'food, drink and fun', or

Dodo Posters

Address: 1st Floor, Alfie's Antique Market, 13-25 Church St, NW8
Hours: Tues-Sat 10:30-17:30
Telephone: 020 7706 1545
Web: www.alfiesantiques.com
Tube/rail: Edgware Rd/Marylebone
Bus: 139, 189

pretty much everything apart from travel and film. The walls are covered with famous brand names, many long since vanished from the shops: beauties from 'Lux' admire their stockinged legs, cheery polar bears tuck in to their Eldorado ice cream, whilst the Bisto Kids are as appetized as ever by the smell of that gravy.

The stock concentrates on the 1920s and 1930s, with underrated British designers well represented, along with the sought-after Italian and French. A poster by Savignac from the 1930s still surprises today with its bold, almost abstract designs, so clearly influenced by big-name movements such as cubism and futurism. In fact, a jog through Liz's stock is nothing short of an alternative history of modern art.

Prices are very affordable: £60 will secure

Marketing aluminium in the 30s

something (4x3ft), unbacked, and in tip-top condition. Larger items, such as Bellenger's 1936 design for 'Bourin' (7x5ft) go for more like £500, and you should expect to add another £150 for linen backing. Iconic, much reproduced images such as Cappiello's absinthe-loving *Green Devil*, or Gilroy's Guinness ads, can sell for up to £1000. Also on offer are tins, boxes and 'show cards' on stiff cardboard that once stood on counters or hung from ceilings. Among her current favourites Liz includes a 1934 design by Cassandre that was used to decorate the menus of Prunier, the restaurant in Paris. A much larger version can be seen in the Met! If you see something you like, buy it now, as you may not get another chance. After all, it's a miracle these quintessentially ephemeral things are even here in the first place.

If Aladdin had been Italian and lived in the 1960s, then this, without a doubt, would have been his cave. Francesca presides over an enormous variety of items, each testifying to her impeccable taste. Furniture and lighting hold centre stage, whilst around the major pieces is an ever-changing array of ceramics, art, and even a case or two of superb costume jewellery. Regular customers return again and again to keep abreast of the latest discoveries, whilst first-time visitors can hardly fail to enjoy the rush of colour and the great forests of futuristic shapes.

Francesca Martire

Address: 1st Floor, Alfie's Antique Market, 13-25 Church St, NW8
Hours: Tues-Sat 10:00-18:00
Telephone: 020 772 4802
Web: www.alfiesantiques.com
Tube/rail: Edgware Rd/Marylebone
Bus: 139, 189

Most eye-catching of all are the lights that populate the floors, walls, tabletops and ceilings. 'Stil Novo' designs radiate 1950s fun and adventure, whilst a huge, orbiting, multicoloured life-form turns out to be a 1960s take on the classic 'Sputnik' chandelier. Magistretti's glowing, opalescent table lamps meanwhile sprout up beneath 'Atomic' ceiling lights by Valenti, and chandeliers by Sottsas. The furniture is no less exciting, with early 1950s cabinets by Paolo Buffa or a chest of drawers by Gio Ponti, all set off to perfection by 'Fontana Arte' mirrors and prints by Vasarely. Some of Francesca's own favourites are tucked away among the costume jewellery, which is mostly of the rich, romantic variety and includes major names such as Dior.

Every one of these lovely objects is a pleasure to behold, but their rarity comes

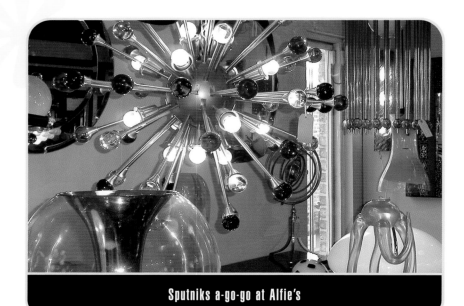

Sputniks a-go-go at Alfie's

at a price. The more spectacular lights can cost several thousand pounds, whilst museum-quality furniture from the pre-war years has been known to break the £20k barrier. Time to dig down the back of the sofa!

Every so often I walk into a shop where I simply want to buy the lot: lock, stock and retro barrel. And so it is with Vincenzo Cafarella, specialists in Italian design from the 1940s to the 1970s. Here you'll find furniture, glass and ceramics by all the major names from Gio Ponti and Seguso to Sottsass and Venini. But most of all it's the spectacular display of lighting that attracts enthusiasts from all over the world.

Vincenzo Cafarella

Address: Ground Floor, Alfie's Antique Market, 13-25 Church St, NW8
Hours: Tues-Sat 10:00-18:00
Telephone: 020 7724 3701
Web: www.vinca.co.uk
Tube/rail: Edgware Rd/Marylebone
Bus: 139, 189 139, 189

Current star of the show is an elaborate, sculptural wall-light by Mazzega, with fourteen bulbs secreted among 85 iridescent discs. Above it hangs a chandelier in the form of a huge descending spiral made from chrome chains and glass strips; whilst over in the corner, next to the pair of lime-green 1950s armchairs, is a domed-glass floor-lamp by Mangiarotti. *Wow!* Everywhere you look there are futuristic creations as bold and breathtaking as they are famous. The effect is like being on the set of *Barbarella*!

Vincenzo and colleague Monica have long championed these amazing styles and designs. Their love for the shapes, colours and sheer originality of the pieces they sell is highly infectious. Expect to pay £2,500 for a late 1960s Mazzega chandelier in thick glass with vivid, acid-etched colouring, and around £1,500 for a Fontana Arte glass-topped coffee table. Murano vases are perennial bestsellers, and continue to influence contemporary design. Among Monica's furniture favourites is an early 1970s semi-sculptured coffee-table made from eighteen separate pieces of curved steel. These can be slotted together to form one huge table, or three smaller ones, or you can dot them about the place as stand-alone pieces. Either way, they look great and are yours for £1,200.

Italian design at its best

With glossy mags ever keener to feature post-war Italian designs in fashion shoots and interiors, so customers are becoming increasingly discerning. These days couples, collectors and celebrities all compete for these beautiful and dramatic items.

Apparently Peter Sellers was an avid fan of vintage hi-fi, and a recent bio-pic shows him admiring his collection. If you happen to see the film, just remember that all those lovely boxes with the shiny knobs on were hired from London's unique Vintage Wireless Company. The shop is tucked away in a side street just off the Edgware Road, and from a distance could easily be mistaken for a run-of-the-mill radio shack. Nothing could be further from the truth! Since 1979 owner Bob (aka Mr Sayed) has presided over a superb assortment of vintage turntables, radiograms, wirelesses, dansettes, reel-to-reels, amps and mikes.

Vintage Wireless London

Address: 17 Bell St, NW1
Hours: Mon-Fri 10:00-17:00, Sat 10:30-16:00
Telephone: 020 7258 3448
www.vintagewirelesslondon.co.uk
Tube/rail: Edgware Rd
Bus: 6, 16, 98, 414

Among his current favourites is a space-age turntable made by cult brand 'Transcriptor' in the early 1970s, and which makes an appearance in *Clockwork Orange*. Also commanding attention is the Wondergram from the early 1960s, which wins the prize for the world's smallest record player. Hardly bigger than a cigarette case (and even styled like one), it can just about accommodate the radius of a 7in single: cute! One more must-see is the 1930s wireless made for London Transport's staff canteens. The speaker mesh is in the shape of the London Underground symbol , whilst the back is modelled on a double-decker bus. It's quite superb, it's £350, and it's impossible to imagine any present-

Deco with knobs on

day transport operator going to that amount of trouble.

Items range from the 1930s to the 1980s, and include everything from designs for Braun by Dieter Rams to ever popular Dansettes and even the legendary circular radios made by Ecko in the 40s.

All the machines are fully working, thanks to Bob's expert restorations: he's one of a select few who not only know how to fix the vintage electrics, but have the spare parts to do so. Customers from all over the globe come here for the stunning designs, or for that special sound that only valves and early transistors can make.

EUSTON

'P op' is the word at Planet Bazaar, where the stock is fun, futuristic and in full technicolour. Since opening in the mid-1990s the store has become a place of pilgrimage for those who like their materials man-made rather than organic. Moulded plastics and fibreglass are the order of

Planet Bazaar

Address: 149 Drummond St, NW1
Hours: Mon-Sat 11:30-19:00
Telephone: 020 77387 8326 / 07956 326301
Web: www.planetbazaar.co.uk
Tube/rail: Euston/Euston Sq
Bus: 10, 18, 30, 73, 205, 390

the day, along with a whole raft of other day-glo synthetics.

The furniture comes in a wide variety of once-radical, now-iconic shapes, such as trademark Panton chairs or the same designer's beautiful cone-shaped seating from the late 1950s. Also on offer are Olivier Mourgue's Djinn-series sofas, as immortalized in the space-station sequence of 2001, and yours to take home for around £1600. For all her obvious love of bold, forward-looking designs, owner Maureen Silverman is far from dogmatic about styles or dates, so in among the Eames, Nelson and Bertoia you might also find an occasional piece of early Aalto, or even an English rosewood sideboard by Merrow Associates.

Every bit as important as what's standing on the floor of Planet Bazaar is what's hanging on the walls. Art is a real strong point, with Jamie Reid a perennial favourite along with Vasarely (typically £800 a print). Peter Blake's *Babe Rainbow* jostles for space with *Wonder Woman* and portraits by Tretchikoff, whilst towering over them all is a striking life-size picture of John Lennon published by FanFotos in the 1960s. The shop has something for everyone, and for all budgets: classic glassware by Holmgaard and Whitefriars starts from around £60, and another £100 or so will open up a choice of 1970s chairs. If you're not sure how your pad will take to a tangerine sofa or a lamp in pink plastic, then you can always take advantage of Planet Bazaar's interior design service.

HENDON

Packed with character and literally floor-to-ceiling goodies, this is just the type of shop you'd see in some Hollywood fantasy. Audiences would take to the owner (played by Hugh Grant), but remind themselves they'd never see anything like it in real life. Except here it is, and tucked away in far-flung Hendon.

For locals, Talking Machine has been a landmark since 1975, when

The Talking Machine

Address: 30 Watford Way, Hendon NW4
Hours: Best to phone first, but usually Mon-Fri 10:00-16:00, Sat 10:00-13:30
Telephone: 020 8202 3473 / 07774 103139
Web: www.gramophones.ndirect.co.uk
Tube/rail: Hendon Central
Bus: 113, 186

its windows first showcased the gramophones, radios and historic recordings that remain its unique stock-in-trade today. Guaranteed attention-grabbers are the fabulous horns that sprout up from dozens of turntables like fantastic tin flowers. The manufacturers' names are a roll-call of the early days of recorded sound: Pathé, Bettini, Columbia, Bestone, Klingsor and the unforgettable Regal-Zonophone. All models are in perfect working order, even those that pre-date World War I. In those days, chart toppers were still mostly supplied on fragile cylinders, rather than new-fangled flat discs. They were packaged in quaint cardboard tubes, and often sported a picture of Edison on the side. Talking Machine always carries a stock of these rare cylinders, so the proud new owner of an antique phonograph can enjoy some actual sounds as well as the lovely machinery; opera arias, music hall ditties and highland flings, all in tubular format, tend to sell for around £25–£35 each.

Less exotic, but in their own way just as beautiful, are the gramophones, dating from the turn of the century to as recently as the early 1950s. There are portables, coin-op devices and turntables tucked inside splendid oak cabinets,

Low-fi marvels in Hendon

sometimes disguised as bookshelves, or even a miniature grand piano. Though mostly pre–electrical, there are occasional voltage-driven numbers, such as Dansettes, a handsome radiogram, or even, on my last visit, an AMI Continental jukebox (which some lucky customer was just carting out of the door).

A beautiful 1920s or 1930 apparatus would liven up any room, and might sell for as little as £300 to £400, though collectors happily pay many times that for certain sought-after models. Ask to hear one in action, and you'll be hooked: there's something about the quality of the sound as it emerges from those horns – low-fi, yes, but bold, too, and quite glorious. Owner David Smith always stocks a huge range of spare needles and a wide assortment of good value 78s. As for volume control, stand by with a spare sock — it works wonders.

ISLINGTON

After *Noah*? Surely that's taking retro just a bit *too* far! In fact, the phrase is from Turkey, where it's a handy way of dating something when you haven't a clue how old it is. A fine name, therefore, for a shop that doesn't limit its stock to any one particular time or place. What matters instead is that the owners really *like* the characterful things they sell.

In practice this means a vast and varied selection of items dating from around 1880 to the present day. Some of the furniture is antique, but much is

After Noah

Address: 121 Upper St, N1
Hours: Mon-Sat 10:00-18:00, Sun 12:00-17:00
Telephone: 020 7359 4281
Web: www.afternoah.com
Tube/rail: Angel/Essex Rd
Bus: 4, 19, 30, 43
Branch: 261 King's Rd, SW3
Hours: As for Upper St

from the 1930s to the 1950s (and occasionally later). The clean-lined Heal's aesthetic is prominent here, as well as a robust, functional, even Utility feel to many of the pieces on show. Given the eclectic, ever-changing mix, the prices can vary enormously. The single most expensive item ever sold was a complete 1950s kitchen with every one of its units in perfect condition, which went for a staggering £5,000! More typically you might find a chest of drawers for £300–£500, or lampshades, Lovats vases, anglepoise lamps (£180) and huge clocks that would not be out of place above a railway platform. There's also kitchenware, lovely fans with metal grills and propeller blades, and a whole host of 'things you can't immediately think of a purpose for' – not forgetting seasonal changes too, with vintage toys headlining in the run-up to Christmas.

After Noah aims to give its customers the complete package, so when they fall in love with an oak table or a brushed aluminium dresser they'll also find all the little extras that will set it off to perfection. Fans include local theatre and television folk, shopfitters, young professionals, and those who just pop in when they fancy a jelly baby.

A feature on the Holloway Road since 1985, 'Back in Time' ranks as one of London's more venerable post-war design specialists. Owners Mario and Paul keep the large, single room well stocked with items dating from the 1950s to the present day. Characterful originals are mixed with high quality remakes, the designs

Back In Time

Address: 93 Holloway Rd, N7
Hours: Mon–Sat 10:00—18:00
Telephone: 020 7700 0744 / 07956 827589
Web: www.backintimeuk.com
Tube/rail: Highbury & Islington
Bus: 43, 271, 393

tending to be from the US and Europe rather than the UK. Among the earlier items are 1950s kitchen units in brushed aluminium, along with sympathetic table lamps and some Danish classics such as teak dining chairs and chests of drawers (£200–£400). All are very much of their time, as is Pierre Paulin's 1967 'tongue chair', which makes a distinctly anatomical shape from its stretch fabric and steel frame.

Modern re-runs are all manufactured under licence and include Eames chairs (by Vitra), as well as the iconic 'Grand Confort' sofa by Le Corbusier in tubular steel and leather (£950). Also new, but a real standout, is the famous 'ball chair' originally designed by Eero Arnio in 1966 and here presented in a host of unique variations. All feature full 360-degree movement, allowing the chair to move on

Eero Arnio's Ball chair

its base like an eye in a socket. Customers can specify their preferred frame colour and cushion fabric (from day-glo to fake fur), and can also have discreet internal speakers. The whole package is yours for £2000, and is cosy enough to sub-let.

Gone are the days when passers-by would pop in and say 'my mum had one of those'. These last few years have seen an explosion of interest in post-war design, which has brought about an ever-growing number of specialist shops and ever-more design-savvy clientèle. Of course, back in the 1960s

Fandango

Address: 50 Cross St, N1
Hours: Tues-Sat 11:00-18:00
Telephone: 020 7226 1777 / 07979 650805
Web: www.fandango.uk.com
Tube/rail: Angel/Essex Rd
Bus: 4, 19, 30, 38, 43, 56, 341,

and 1970s only a *very* special mum had a house filled with classic Italian and Scandinavian design. But today there are a great many people who would like their living rooms to look as elegant and chic as the interior of Fandango.

Owners Jonathan and Henrietta have been in Islington for nearly five years, and have a following among style-conscious homemakers who share their love for all things refined, graceful and modern – in a mid-century sort of way. Among Jonathan's current favourites is a late 1940s wooden chair by Jorgen Baekmark (£650). Its extra-wide seat and graceful curved frame give it an eye-catching profile, whilst the high quality of the joinery makes it a perfect marriage of modern sensibility and Danish craft tradition.

If we look to the Scandinavians for the best in woodwork, then it's the Italians we turn to when it comes to lighting. Some of the best examples are the chandeliers by Mazzega. The glass is of the highest quality, and great care went into their manufacture. Of the three or four examples on display, pride of place goes to one with panels of opalescent glass slotted together to form one huge, bulbous shape that looks like it's made of soap bubbles. There are also ceiling lights by StilNovo, shades by Vistosi, classic 'sputnik' lamps, and a 'pistillo' or two for good measure. These last are named after part of a flower, but evoke a kind of space-age vegetation only the 1960s could have dreamt up.

When you hear the word 'Jukebox' there's a good chance the first thing you'll think of will be the Wurlitzer '1015', often taken as a symbol of all things 1950s, but in fact first produced as early as 1946. Its classic arched top frames the turntable like a little stage – complete with mock curtain – whilst the massive speaker cabinet is bathed in a uniquely

Jukebox London

Address: Colebrooke Row, London N1
Hours: Phone to view
Telephone: 020 7713 7668
Web: www.jukeboxlondon.co.uk
Tube/rail: Angel
Bus: 4, 43, 153, 205, 214, 274, 394

warm and sugary glow. The design is iconic – copied everywhere – but if you want to be one of the lucky few to own the real thing, then David Webb is the man to see. Ask him nicely and he'll even open up the 1015's casing so you can watch the elegant record-changing mechanism in glorious action, or see the tiny heaters that excite the bubbles in the multicoloured, oil-filled tubes. There is the small matter of price, which at £12,500 does make for a serious investment. But don't forget that you're buying a piece of history, and one that's been lovingly restored: as much as half the asking price might already have been spent on period-perfect parts and materials.

If you don't have enough 78s to fill the '1015', then for £7500 why not try the Wurlitzer '1700' instead. Dating from 1954, this was the first model specifically designed to play those new-fangled 45s. Alternatively you could take a look at something by a different manufacturer: in recent years David has seen the market broaden considerably, and his stock now typically includes examples from all the legendary jukebox companies, such as Rockola, Seeberg and AMI (who

Inside the Wurlitzer 1015

as Automatic Musical Instruments started the whole thing, back in the late 1920s). Currently in vogue is the AMI Continental II, which for £6500 offers great sound with 'auto-mix' stereo, and is another indisputable masterpiece of design. Put it in the corner of your room, and guests will think you've adopted Robbie the Robot.

Don't have the room? Of course you do – just get rid of the sofa. With '200 selections' to keep you dancing you'll be too busy to sit down, anyway. If you're seriously interested, contact David via the web site and arrange a demo. He no longer operates a shop as such, but stores the machines in a lovely old house in Islington. All the models are ready loaded with fabulous 1950s' and 1960s' vinyl, and will spring to life at the touch of a button. If you think they look good, just wait till you hear them!

M etro Retro has come to occupy a distinctive place in London's vintage design world. Founder Saxon Durrant has always had an eye for the unusual, and a particular taste for the industrial look; as a result he offers a unique array of brushed-steel furniture and 'reclaimed' items.

Much of the fun comes from taking industrial designs and reinventing them as household objects, beginning with favourites such as stripped metal desks, chairs, lockers and filing cabinets

Metro Retro

Address: 1 White Conduit St, Chapel Market, N1
Hours: Thurs-Sat 11:00-18:00
Telephone: 020 7278 4884
Web: www.metroretro.co.uk
Tube/rail: Angel
Bus: 30, 73, 394, 476

all in satin silver-grey finish. For maximum effect, the items to use are those that least disguise their origins, and these include glazed medical cabinets, tubular-steel coatstands, and even some trolleys from a 1930s shoe factory.

Apart from the major furniture and storage items, the functional theme is extended by a host of smaller but equally practical objects, such as 1960s telephones, bakelite school clocks, and enamelled pendant lampshades complete with cast-iron galleries straight out of a pre-war warehouse. A selection of 1970s rosewood sideboards adds a more familiar touch, as do the floor lights by Panton and the smart desktop calendars.

The showroom is a compact hideaway just off the busy Chapel Street market and much of the stock is stored at the company's warehouse in Essex. For updates on latest acquisitions, and to reserve your own slice of shop-floor style, keep an eye on the user-friendly web site.

Origin showcases the very best in modernism, and owner David Tatham is happy to share his passion for the beautiful, clean-lined objects he stocks. All the items are originals, with the emphasis on architect-designed plywood furniture from the 1930s to the 1950s. The shelves and table-tops also sport a selection of Scandinavian ceramics, glass and woodenware, whilst the walls boast an uncommon display of British modernist paintings from the 1950s (£400–£2,000).

Origin

Address: 25 Camden Passage, N1
Hours: Wed 10:00-18:00, Thurs-Fri 12:00-18:00, Sat 10:00-18:00
Telephone: 020 7704 1326
Web: www.origin101.co.uk
Tube/rail: Angel
Bus: 19, 30, 38, 43, 73, 341, 476

There is absolutely nothing run-of-the-mill in this shop, which has the feel of an exclusive gallery and attracts discerning buyers from around the world. Among the most spectacular pieces are a *chaise longue* by Marcel Breuer from 1936, and a walnut screen by Charles and Ray Eames, only in production for a very limited period between 1949 and 1951; these are things one rarely sees outside a museum, and both are on sale for around £7,000—£8,000. By any standards this makes them serious investments, but true landmarks of design don't come cheap, and the pleasure they provide is priceless. For those whose budget is not quite the equal of their taste, the good news is that there's also a selection of simple but elegant plywood chairs that can be had for as little as £100.

For David, the aesthetics of modernism are as valid today as they ever were, so he's loathe to use the word 'retro' – even for something close on 70 years old. What's

Modernist masterpiece from Giuseppe Pagano

beyond dispute is that the treasures on offer at Origin are from the earliest, most formative days of a still-vibrant movement, which extends in scope far beyond the decorative arts. Start off with that single plywood chair and before you know it you'll be wanting to live in a twentieth-century dream house by Richard Neutra or Albert Frey! David's advice is always to 'buy with your eyes' and opt for what you really like, rather than for what you feel you *ought* to like. My advice is: go and enjoy – but don't call it retro!

Vintage clothing fans are spoilt for choice in North London, especially when it comes to 20s beaded dresses, costume jewellery and timeless post-war glamour. The action centres on Islington and Edgware Road but spreads out to Camden, Euston and beyond.

CHALK FARM

At first sight, the Stables Market arches seem to offer one enormous, indivisible mass of second-hand and vintage clothing. But some of the arches are occupied by two or more separate dealers, as is the case at Number 50, where the rear part is home to the highly individual Hula Bop.

Run by Terry for the last three years, this tucked-away gem has one of the best selections of

Hula Bop

Address: Arch 50, Stables Market, Chalk Farm Road, NW1
Hours: Fri-Sun 09:00-17:00
Telephone: 07960 942131
Tube/rail: Chalk Farm/Camden Town
Bus: 24, 27, 31, 168

original 1950s menswear in London. The accent is firmly on cool American styles, and Hawaiian shirts are something of a speciality. Classics from as far back as the 1940s sport truly superb prints of angel fish, South Pacific beauties or tropical birds, and attract serious collectors. Ladies can join in too, with 'cabana' sets and two-pocket female versions, Mexican circle skirts, knitwear, and dresses.

Other standouts include zip-up reversible gabardine jackets – the hepcat's outerwear of choice – along with some fab chunky cardigans, all original, boasting bold designs of yachts and baseball players. Most unusual of all, and highly sought-after, are the military 'tour' jackets, as worn by the US Forces in the 1950s and 1960s. Their back panels are embroidered with huge dragons, or maps accompanied by legends such as Born to Battle or Viet Nam Okinawa 1967–8. For fans of military gear there are even some WWII items to cut a GI dash. Customers are a mix of the hardcore rockin' crowd and confident, younger guys (or gals) who know a design classic when they see it. If you want authentic 1950s cuts – rather than the cartoon versions – then this is a great place to start looking.

Expand your horizons and vary your hemlines at the irresistible
Biba Lives (see page 87)

B rightening up the northern end of Chalk Farm Road, Modern Age is a colourful outpost on Camden's vintage clothing trail. Almost facing it is legendary venue, The Roundhouse, one-time home to punk pandemonium and psychedelic jelly-throwing freak-outs. For better or worse, the music has moved on, but at Modern Age the fashions of those rebellious decades can still be found in abundance.

Modern Age Vintage Clothing

Address: 65 Chalk Farm Rd, NW1
Hours: Daily 10:30-18:00
Telephone: 020 7482 3787
Web: www.modern-age.co.uk
Tube/rail: Chalk Farm
Bus: 24, 27, 31, 168

Prices tend to be at the lower end of the spectrum, and appeal to a generally younger, under-30s crowd. Items from the 1950s start from as little as £25 for a classic floral day dress, whilst the more elaborate evening numbers with details in lace or embroidery sell for around £40–£50. Equally tempting are the sleeveless 1960s dresses in bright, abstract designs and some fabulous tapestry coats – very Jean Shrimpton. There's also a good line in outrageous full-length 1970s gowns that will transport you straight to Abigail's party. The assortment of bags is always worth investigating, with 1970s items and clutch bags starting from £10, and occasional pieces from the 1950s selling at around £30. Menswear makes a larger splash than average and takes up about half the floor space: 1970s patterned shirts are a strong point, as are jackets in velvet and suede and also the huge range of trousers, which includes some real party numbers in day-glo prints (£25, and I dare you to wear *those* in Asda!).

Original 70s platforms

The other major attraction of Modern Age is its hire stock, the larger part of which is kept at a nearby warehouse. A truly vast collection awaits groups of friends, or theatre and film companies, who book a viewing in advance. There are high quality outfits from the 1920s to the 1960s, with a particularly strong line in 1950s glamour (a personal favourite of owners, Julia and Steven) and a beautiful range of vintage wedding dresses (see web site for pictures). You might even recognize some of the dresses and woollen suits that were used in the film *Evita*.

There's a smaller hire section at the back of the shop (very good for the 1970s), and prices range from £25–£40 for one week's use, inclusive of all cleaning. You can also hire any of the items on sale, which is a good way of 'test driving' something you're not sure about. A dress on sale for £30 will hire at £10, and if you fall in love with it, all you have to do is phone up and tell them to keep the £20 deposit. Couldn't be easier! A great place to experiment, have fun, and perhaps pick up a bargain.

EDGWARE ROAD

Nicknamed Biba since school, owner Sonia has hand-chosen every item in this beautiful collection of clothing, and it shows. For 1950s fans there are dozens of gorgeous, super-fashionable cocktail dresses in elegant silks, and layered, pastel chiffons. Many boast exquisite details such as trailing bows, lace overlays or embroidered flowers, and some come with matching bolero jackets or capes. Yes, at last you really *can* be Grace Kelly ('High Society' that is, not 'High

Biba Lives

Address: Alfie's Antique Market, 13-25 Church St, NW8
Hours: Tues-Sat 10:00-18:00
Telephone: 020 7258 7999
Web: www.bibalives.com
Tube/rail: Edgware Rd/Marylebone
Bus: 139, 189

Noon'!). Prices for these average £80 to £90, but can be £200 or more for something really special. Equally exciting are the rails of 1960s items, priced around £40 and including dropped-waist day-dresses, classic suits and to-die-for sleeveless mini-dresses in swirling, psychedelic prints (just the thing for a trip on the scooter). There's menswear too, with jackets, suits and a good selection of shirts for around £20).

A unique touch is the Biba Lives label sewn into every garment. This further heightens the shop's contemporary, almost designer feel, and helps extend its appeal to many who might not have bought vintage before. In fact, the superb condition of the clothes has had some customers thinking they were straight off the catwalk. There are hats and bags to complete the perfect outfit, and everything on show is also available for hire. A top-of-the-range, full-length gown costing £100–£500 to buy, hires out at £35 for one night (£10 for each night extra). Smaller items, including most of the dresses, suits and skirts, hire for £10 a day (inclusive of dry cleaning).

You will occasionally find original 'Biba' items or something by Ossie Clarke, but it's the designs that matter here, not the labels (apart from their own, of course). Current stock reflects the huge demand for the 1950s silhouette – with skirts 'the bigger the better' – but the focus may change depending on whatever becomes the next big thing. What *won't* change is the quality, condition and all-round fair pricing of the clothes on offer. If you leave empty-handed, then you haven't looked properly!

F rom outside, Cristobal looks like a regular antique shop. But make your way past the gilt mirrors, and you'll suddenly find yourself standing amidst one of London's most spectacular displays of vintage costume jewellery. Take a deep breath, pick up your jaw, and settle down to admire the exquisite designs by Dior and Schiaparelli, a Miriam Haskell three-rope necklace or a brooch by Wallis Simpson's favourite, Stanley Haggler.

Cristobal

Address: 26 Church St, NW8
Hours: Tues-Sat 10:00-17:00
Telephone: 020 7724 7230
Web: www.cristobal.co.uk
Tube/rail: Edgware Rd/Marylebone Rd
Bus: 139, 189

Customers from all over the globe (including the Thai royal family) return again and again to this beautiful shop, which also supplied the sparklies for Madonna in Evita. Newcomers are equally welcome, and owners Steven, Kevin and Yai will

The glittering wonderland that is Cristobal

be only too glad to introduce you to the wonders of the costume jewellery world. Many who have tip-toed through the door with a vague idea of buying something 'a little different' have emerged four hours later with a fully formed passion.

Stock is mostly from the 1940s or 1950s, though you might find an occasional nugget of Victoriana, or even a piece from as late as the 1980s, if it has sufficient character. Prices range from less than £20 (for a pair of earrings) up to around £1500 for a classic Chanel necklace still in its original box. It's worth remembering that some of these items were not exactly cheap when they were first produced ($25 was a lot of money in the 1930s), but for the modern buyer there's the added appeal that no one else is likely to be wearing the same thing at a party. Among the large and ever-changing stock you can usually find pieces by 'Joseph of Hollywood', whose trademark bronzed, non-reflective surfaces were designed to look a million dollars when worn on screen by the stars of black-and-white movies. A large acorn and oak-leaf brooch as modelled by Jane Russell sells for around £250 (and that's not a lot of money to look like Jane Russell!).

Collectors come in search of all the big names or perhaps a particular theme, such as insects, birds or those neat little brooches shaped like Christmas trees. But most of all these lovely creations demand to be worn. Certainly it takes some courage to wear one of the more fanciful Carmen Miranda numbers, but you don't have to go the whole way: every piece is a celebration of life. Chances are that, when you buy that little splash of colour to set against your safe old Prada, you'll soon be thinking it's the best purchase you've ever made.

You can hardly miss the spectacular displays of clothing and homewares conjured up by proprietors of 'The Girl Can't Help it', Sparkle Moore and Cad van Swankster (aka Jasja). It's a delight simply to wander between the different stands and watch the scene shift from rat-pack bachelor pad to Jayne Mansfield's boudoir, and on again to what could be Doris Day's travel trunk.

The large selection of menswear is mostly from the 1940s and 1950s, and all of it very cool in a sleek, LA-hotshot sort of way. One great thing about men's clothes from these

The Girl Can't Help It

Address: Ground Floor, Alfie's Antique Market, 13-25 Church St, NW8
Hours: Tues-Sat 10:30-17:30
Telephone: 020 7724 8984
Web: www.sparklemoore.com
Tube/rail: Edgware Rd/Marylebone
Bus: 139, 189

decades is that many of the styles have never been recycled by subsequent eras. Take the 'Hollywood', a kind of roomy, lightweight jacket, often sporting smart little details such as full-length darts, suede inserts, or two-tone panels on the shoulders. This is the sort of sharp and confident outfit that has never been exactly mainstream, and the price today (£200–£300) reflects sheer scarcity as much as the unique look. The 1950s gabardine shirts are also emphatically of their era, and top quality too, as are the short, zip-front reversible jackets.

Sparkle's superb womenswear is mostly of a similar age, and with an emphasis very much on glamour rather than daywear. Shelves of shoes – sandals, wedges, mules and slingbacks – are arranged with sympathetic hats and handbags, whilst nearby rails positively buzz with a kaleidoscopic profusion of full-skirt 1950s party dresses. There are hand-painted Mexican circle-skirts (£80–£250), frothy petticoats, girdles, Hawaiian halter-necks and a well picked selection of costume jewellery.

Everything is original, including the highly popular sets of glasses sporting classic Elvgren pin-ups (far better quality than the cheap reproductions). There's nothing here that Sparkle and Jasja wouldn't wear themselves or have in their own home (which, by the way, is something to behold!). The customer list is a who's who of the film, media and fashion world, but more than anything else this is a shop for people who appreciate well made, top quality and perennially stylish clothing. Jasja's timeless advice is not to be afraid to stand out, and whatever look you choose, to be sure to make it your own.

P ersiflage manages to pack an enormous amount of character into a far from cavernous space. First to grab the attention are the main rails of carefully selected womenswear, with lovely examples of 1930s and 1940s dresses in georgette and *crêpe de chine*. These come in shimmering full-length styles as well as shorter, day-time varieties, and are joined by 1950s cotton print tops, tailored jackets and – to complete the wardrobe – even a selection of coats, silk robes and peignoirs.

Persiflage

Address: 2nd Floor Front, Alfie's Antique Market, 13-25 Church St, NW8
Hours: Tues-Sat 10:30-17:45
Telephone: 020 7724 7366
Tube/rail: Edgware Rd/Marylebone
Bus: 139, 189

What soon becomes clear is that much of Persiflage's stock is on an altogether smaller scale, and tucked away in polished wooden drawers. A towering cabinet opens to reveal a rich assortment of buttons, beads, cottons, lace and silks, some with a story to tell. Not so long ago, owner

'Of course I deserve it!'

Gwyneth had the fortune and good sense to buy up the remnants of the famed Hartnell beading atelier, and is now the proud holder of thousands of sequins and beautiful bits and bobs which she's gradually parcelling out by the half dozen. Mum's button box was never as good as this! The sewing ancillaries extend to a useful collection of *How To...* books, whilst the sizeable range of knitting patterns is proving ever more popular with a 20-something, stitch-happy crowd (look out for them in your local!). Also on offer are shelves full of fabrics that would look as good hanging on a wall as covering a shapely back. Gwyneth has a real eye, too, for quirkier items, such as masks, veils and even the occasional belly dancer's costume.

The prices are extremely good, with many of the dresses at around £20 and blouses more like £8. Not surprisingly the turnover is high, so it always pays to pop back for an update. Gwyneth is also part-owner of Islington's 'Past Caring', where she spends a part of each week. If she's not at Alfie's when you visit, then long-term colleague Ruth will be there to offer all the assistance you need at this small but perfectly formed treat.

A bsolutely nothing to do with that Belgian cartoon character, this is in fact one of London's more remarkable vintage clothing specialists. Lesley and Peter have built up, over many years, what is now one of the few truly unmissable destinations for all lovers of 1920s clothing.

Great care is taken to select only the best quality items, which is why Tin Tin can count even museums among its customers. Fortunately for the rest of us, this doesn't mean the prices are prohibitive. Beaded dresses typically sell for £200–£300, which doesn't seem so

Tin Tin Collectables

Address: Ground Floor, Alfie's Antique Market, 13-25 Church St, NW8
Hours: Tues-Sat 10:00-18:00
Telephone: 020 7258 1305
Web: www.tintincollectables.com
Tube/rail: Edgware Rd/Marylebone
Bus: 139, 189

much to pay for something guaranteed to turn every head at a party. And for serious buyers, Lesley will unpack the extra-special stuff, kept boxed up and out of harm's way. Current star of the show is a pristine 'flapper dress', with geometric and floral designs picked out in beads on a pale cream shift.

Whilst Tin Tin's clothing is mostly 1920s, later decades also have their place. Feminine chiffon dresses from the 1930s in classic autumnal prints sell for around £150–£300, and these are always in their original length rather than the common shortened versions. Meanwhile, from the relatively recent 1950s you might find a brocade coat by Hardy Amies (£295) or signature daisy-print separates from Ken Scott. Original Biba dresses sell for around £250. From time to time you'll also find Mary Quant or Zandra Rhodes, and if you don't see what you're after, then make sure to ask – this shop has hidden depths!

Peter and Lesley are true enthusiasts, and will wax lyrical on the many varieties of velvet or the finer details of 1940s handbags (of which there are usually some great examples among their large stock of accessories). Anyone who comes here still doubting the delights of pre-war fashions can't fail to be a convert by the time they leave.

EUSTON

C lothes, records, books – Delta of Venus is not so much a shop as an experience, a way of life even. Welcome to the world of Leigh Wildman and his two 'secret agents', Danny and Lydia, who are in love with the style, the glamour and the good-natured rebellion of the golden years of pop.

The musical references are everywhere: labels on the clothing carry helpful hints on the intended look, which may be early Roxy Music, 1960s garage punk, glam, CBGBs, 1950s rock'n'roll, beatnik chic, or even the 1980s TOTP garb of rah-rah skirts and pixie boots. On shelves around the room, top hats and silver platform shoes conjure up images of Delta's guiding spirits – Bolan, the Sweet, and above all, Bowie. The Thin White One remains a perennial bestseller, with vintage tour items flying off the rails.

The bohemian feel of the shop and its rock'n'roll attitude appeal to a youthful

Delta of Venus

Address: 151 Drummond St, NW1
Hours: Mon–Sat 11:00–19:00
Telephone: 020 7387 3037
Tube/rail: Euston/Euston Square
Bus: 10, 18, 30, 73, 205, 390

Beaton meets Bolan

clientèle. Many customers are in their teens or early 20s and just discovering the styles and sounds of an earlier era, remaking them into something to call their own. The skirts, jackets, jewellery and bags have all been carefully selected, so there's no sense of having to sift through dross to get at the good stuff. Featherweight gypsy dresses from the 1970s go for around £30, as do sequinned cocktail numbers, whilst the most expensive item ever sold was a pair of original 'Sex' label leather trousers from Seditionaries, which fetched £500. Along with the vintage clobber you'll also find fresh and funky new designs self-produced in limited runs – such as shirts adorned with Brian Jones or, the current favourite, Steve Priest of Sweet (the one with the most make-up!) framed by the cheerful words 'Fuck Off'.

Original rock Ts are the latest big thing – 'the more beat up the better'. With names such as Dylan, Floyd and Kiss all back in fashion, perhaps it's even safe to admit that you *do* like ELP. Make no bones about it, I love this shop, and if they did B&B I might well take up residence.

HOLLOWAY ROAD

Long gone are the days when £15 would secure a 1950s cocktail dress or some amazing gabardine shirt. But for those of us who can't afford to chase the prices up it's nice at least to know where our £15 will be best spent – which is pretty much the *raison d'être* of 162, for more than 10 years a beacon of 'shabby chic' out on the Holloway Road.

The shop enjoys a following among those who are short on cash but rich in imagination, and who can manage to look a million dollars for a few quid. When any one style becomes too pricey, owner

162

Address: 162 Holloway Rd, N7
Hours: Mon-Sat 10:00-18:00,
Sun 11:00-18:00
Telephone: 020 7700 2354
Tube/rail: Holloway Rd
Bus: 43, 153, 271, 393

John Scott simply moves on and takes the view that if this means no more Chanel suits, then so be it. What it prompts instead is a huge and ever-changing volume of stock from the 1940s to the present day.

Menswear accounts for roughly 40 per cent of the total, and concentrates on jazzy 1970s shirts, Hawaiians, jackets and jeans. For the women, the rails hold some bargains, such as the 1960s sleeveless brocade dresses (£10–£20), coats for £7–£25, lots of fashionable A-line skirts, and tops from £3. On my last visit there was even a stunning 1970s full-length Pucci-esque number in swirls of raspberry and cream and priced at a mouth-watering £15. Winter months bring forth a selection of 1970s leather coats with long collars and wide lapels, whilst military gear comes and goes fast all year round. If anything hangs around for too long, then its price is gradually reduced. If value and fashion were one and the same, then this would be a couture house, for sure.

ISLINGTON

Annie's shop is so utterly enchanting I can't believe she doesn't charge admission! From the flowers outside to the window displays of summery lawn dresses and sequinned tops, everything is pretty, feminine and timelessly *à la mode*.

The stock concentrates on the 1920s and 1930s, but also includes pieces from as late as the 1950s: think Merchant Ivory meets 'Moulin

Annie's Vintage Costume & Textiles

Address: 12 Camden Passage, Islington, N1
Hours: Mon–Sat 11:00–18:00 (from 09:00 on Wed & Sat)
Telephone: 020 7359 0796 / 0796 803 793
Tube/rail: Angel
Bus: 4, 19, 30, 38, 43, 56, 73, 341, 476

Rouge' by way of 'Mrs Miniver'. Beautiful beaded dresses from the Jazz Age sell for around £350, and a floaty, calf-length chiffon gown will give you a 1930s silhouette for as little as £150. Also on the rails are cotton dresses in classic 1940s prints, devoré jackets, and silk nighties, and the accessories include hats, shoes, and a natty line in crocodile handbags (£50–£80). A sensational arrangement of antique lace announces the increasingly popular bridal collection. With vintage weddings already very chic in the USA, and gowns here in N1 costing as little as £250, there's no excuse for local ring-swappers not to take their cue.

Jazz-age glamour at Annie's

Having been in the business since 1976, Annie has built up a solid-gold reputation and a loyal fan club to match. She has also seen a steady increase in demand for vintage apparel, especially over these last four or five years. As a result, photographers and journalists from all over the world now flock to her for copy and inspiration, whilst customers swear by Annie's as a cutting-edge boutique. Ralph Lauren's bias-cut gowns or Donna Karan's tailored polka dots may have made a splash in all the fashion mags, but true connoisseurs come straight here for the 1930s and 1940s originals (and also save themselves some serious pocket money in the process). Whatever your chosen decade or your not-so-optional budget, you can't fail to enjoy a visit to this unique and delightful dressing-up box. Combine it with a trip to nearby Cloud Cuckoo Land and Eclectica for an afternoon's perfect retail therapy.

I wonder if there's a collective noun for 1920s beaded dresses: a 'stitch' perhaps, or a 'flap'? The word would certainly come in handy in that corner of Islington where Cloud Cuckoo Land competes with nearby Annie's to stock the most – and best – of these beautiful, hand-

Cloud Cuckoo Land

Address: 6 Charlton Place, Camden Passage, Islington, N1
Hours: Mon-Sat 11:00-17:00
Telephone: 020 7354 3141
Tube/Rail: Angel
Bus: 4, 19, 30, 38, 43, 56, 73, 341, 476

sewn confections. Owner Chrissie Harper has run this delightful shop for the last two decades, over which time she has built up a loyal following. The virtues of wearing

50s bags in sculpted lucite

vintage are also perfectly advertised by her colleague Dawn, who always looks so cool in her natty jazz-age ensembles.

Banks of clothing line the cosy first room where the picture rail helps display the more spectacular and often very delicate items in brocade, lace and velvet. The stock is focused on the inter-war years, but also includes later items up to the 1950s. The huge selection of blouses includes trim, tailored designs from the 1930s and 1940s, with fabric-covered buttons and period-perfect peplums, as well as 1950s floral prints in silk and cotton (£25). On neighbouring rails hang 1940s swing jackets (£20–£45) and day dresses for around £50–£60. Every so often you'll find yourself picking up unique older items that are not so easy to put back down: for example, that Edwardian jacket in silk taffeta: surely it has your name on it, as does the lawn dress in classic white muslin (£90, and I won't tell a soul).

At the upper end of the price range are the more delectable numbers from the 1920s, such as superb velvet shawls or a dress of richly coloured beadwork on sheer black chiffon (£350–£500). A simpler but still eye-catching 1920s dress can sell for as little as £225, which means you'll still have some cash left over to put towards your Hispano-Suiza.

A particular strength is Chrissie's collection of handbags, including beautiful examples in sculpted lucite from the 1940s and 1950s that sell for £50—£150, depending on the craftsmanship. Perennial favourites are the 1960s bags by Enid Collins, of which Cloud Cuckoo Land has long been a champion: a typical design in wood with floral decoration sells for around £60—£70.

Men are not overlooked, with a notable collection of 1940s ties selling for around £20 each, along with scarves and 'Beau Brummel' dead-stock shirts. For the budding seamstress (or seamster?) there's even a good selection of patterns from Butterick and Vogue, offering you the chance to find out for yourself just how to make the perfect suit, skirt or shirtwaister. If you don't see what you're after, then make sure that you ask, as there's more stock tucked away. Designers and fashion scouts are dropping by all the time, which means that Cloud Cuckoo's regulars can be sure of staying ahead of the game.

Some of the most alluring examples of vintage costume jewellery can be found at Islington's Eclectica, a charming showcase of a shop just off Camden Passage.

The genre's more flamboyant examples are here passed over in favour of items that are colourful, light-hearted and always very wearable. All are displayed on open shelves

Eclectica

Address: 2 Charlton Place, Islington, N1
Hours: Mon—Sat 11:00–18:00 (from 09:00 on Wed & Sat)
Telephone: 020 7226 5625
Web: www.eclectica.biz
Tube/rail: Angel
Bus: 4, 19, 30, 38, 43, 56, 73, 341

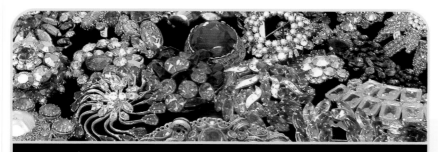

Forget diamonds: make some new best friends at Eclectica

to encourage trying on. Among the older pieces are such pre-war beauties as crystal teardrop necklaces, Edwardian earrings, or strings of Czechoslovakian opaque glass in bright little buttons like smarties. Fans of the 1950s meanwhile will find a wealth of designs from costume's undisputed golden age, including Miriam Haskell's trademark pearls and classics by Trifari. On all sides, the stock sparkles and winks in a way that is wholly seductive. Starbursts of clear pink crystal compete for our attention with faux fruit and feathers of diamante, whilst beneath them is a necklace made from glass the colour of the aurora borealis. Elsewhere, lines of brooches in ruby reds or turquoise blues border whole gardens of frozen blooms, from single daisies and forget-me-nots in wreaths to miniature bouquets tied with little enamelled bows.

Prices are excellent, with pairs of 1930s earrings or 1950s necklaces averaging around £60–£70, the brooches more like £20–£30, and only a few real collectables (such as the ever-popular Haskells) pushing up into three figures. 'Eclectica' also offers a sizeable selection of bags – hand, clutch or evening – from the 1930s to the 1960s, and these enjoy a high turnover (so it's always worth dropping by for an update). Owner Liz travels extensively in search of new treasures; she never buys in bulk but likes everything in the shop to be hand picked. She's built up quite a following, and one glance at this lovely giant jewel-box is enough to see why.

S ugar Antiques is two shops in one, with honours shared between husband and wife Elayne and Tony. Elayne's contribution is a stunning assortment of vintage costume jewellery, including a display of brooches that covers an entire wall. First-time customers often let out an involuntary gasp when confronted by the

Sugar Antiques

Address: 8-9 Pierrepoint Arcade, Camden Passage, Islington, N1
Hours: Wed 06:30-16:30, Sat 09:00-16:00
Telephone: 020 7354 996 / 07973 179980
Web: www.sugarantiques.com
Tube/rail: Angel
Bus: 19, 30, 38, 43, 73, 341

glittering ranks of button-sized cats, butterflies, lizards and stylized Christmas trees.

Classic 1950s pieces are here aplenty, but so too are less common items such as filigree brooches with superb hand-crafted metalwork. Made in Czechoslovakia in the 1920s, these also boast the highest quality glass in subtle and seductive tones, and Elayne is proud to offer one of the best collections in the country (priced from £20–£150). The treasures on display are joined by a whole lot more waiting out of sight: twenty trays of earrings, great thickets of necklaces, and rings by the thousand. Compacts, too, are well represented, with gorgeous glam-era numbers in enamel or burnished gold demanding a place in every fashionable handbag.

Tony presides over a selection of restored fountain pens, lighters and vintage watches, all of which would sharpen the style of any man about town. The pens date from about 1900 to 1970, and the majority are classic Parkers from the 1950s and 1960s. A Parker 51 or a 'Vacuumatic' will cost from £50–£150, whilst a few pennies more will secure a stunning 1928 'Lucky Curve' in 'tango orange'.

Treat your bag to a compact

Pocket watches start from £50 and include all the big names – Rolex, Omega and Longines. Designs range from the intricacies of a Breitling 'Navitimer' to deco faces from the 1930s/1940s, and the space-age, sunburst dials of the early 1970s. Standouts include a very rare, outsized navigator's watch once issued by the Luftwaffe. Small in size, but large in character, 'Sugar' is an integral part of the Islington retro trail (note that it opens on Wednesdays and Saturdays only).

MUSWELL HILL

Once the preserve of the radical few, tattoos have long since joined the mainstream. All the more reason, when you do go under the needle, to get yourself jazzed up with something truly special. Connoisseurs of late have been showing a renewed taste for vintage designs from the 1940s and 1950s, when

New Wave Tattoo Studio

Address: 157 Sydney Rd, Muswell Hill, N10
Hours: Mon–Fri 10:30-17:30, Sat 09:30-16:30
Telephone: 020 8444 8779
Web: www.lalhardy.co.uk
Tube/rail: Bounds Green
Bus: 43, 134

Sailor Jerry...

...and friend!

modern body art was first finding its distinctive attitude and shape. Sailor Jerry Collins out in Hawaii was developing his bold trademark style, whilst all across mainland USA, soon-to-be-iconic images of girls, cars, guitars and dice were pinning down for ever the look and style of post-war, street-wise cool. Here in 1950s Britain such images were exotic indeed, but for most of us today they capture perfectly the unique spirit of the time. And one of the very few places to get your own birthday suit embellished with some authentic 1950s designs is Lal Hardy's world-famous parlour in leafy Muswell Hill.

Believe it or not, the area has something of a reputation (check out the early episode of *Porridge*, where Fletch boasts of having been 'king of the Muswell Hill Teds'). The rockin' crowd from all over the world has long made a bee-line to this legendary place, where they turn canvas for skin art of the highest order. The list of fellow pilgrims ranges from Liam Gallagher and All Saints, to Steps, Liberty X and a whole host of wised-up taste hounds from every imaginable quarter. Lal himself has been here since 1979, and for much of that time has been assisted by Martin Clarke, one of the world's true specialists in 'fifties flash'. A pin-up in the style of Sailor J will need a good few hours' work and will set you back around £75 minimum – and more for a classic by Elvgren. The massive portfolio of available designs covers everything from old favourites such as Sun record labels, swallows and hotrods, to new-fangled kanji, tribal markings and fetish pics.

Whilst you're getting yourself inked you might catch a flying visit by Ritchie Gee, promoter of the nearby Tennessee Club. He often brings visiting acts down for an impromptu jam, and musical guests have included Robert Gordon, Mac Curtis and even Paul Burlison of the original Rock'n'Roll Trio. If there's no live music, then you can always take a look at Lal's priceless scrapbooks, which document the 1970s rock'n'roll revival in all its glorious, greasy detail. Booking is essential, as Lal and Martin are busy every day. Can you wonder at it? This is one of those cultural landmarks that goes beyond mere fame, and stakes its place in myth.

STOKE NEWINGTON

Ribbons & Taylor not only puts Stoke Newington on the retro map, but is a deservedly popular shop where even on a Wednesday afternoon customers drop by in a steady stream to check out the fast-changing stock. One reason for this success is the pricing, which appeals to fashionable locals as well as vintage fans from far and wide. The most you will ever pay for something here is around £75, which would secure a spectacular 1950s evening dress or a full-length leather coat. Just as enticing is the eclectic mix of items that owners Sue and Mort carefully tailor to suit their customers' tastes. The changing seasons also have an impact, with a huge range of cashmere sweaters marking the approach of winter.

Ribbons & Taylor

Address: 157 Stoke Newington Church St, N16
Hours: Tues-Sat 11:00-18:00 (till 19:30 on Thurs), Sun 12:00-17:00
Telephone: 020 7254 4735
Tube/rail: Stoke Newington
Bus: 73, 393, 476

An unusual but perennially popular feature is the selection of leather biker jackets, both men's and women's, and for which R&T has built up a reputation (£26–£45). Menswear generally makes a good showing (about 40 per cent of the total), whilst for the women there are colourful circle skirts, shoes, big net petticoats, and a wide variety of tops (£9–£15). Dresses average £30–£50, and even at the cheaper end of the range you might pick up something as glamorous as a 1960s satin two-piece with pale pink shift and matching bolero jacket. As if this wasn't value enough, the annual sale takes place in August, so make a note in your diary now.

The shop itself has a lovely relaxed ambience with super-friendly staff and good taste in background music (cajun, calypso and jazz). From time to time something really out of the ordinary shows up, such as an amazing 1930s quilted jacket and matching ankle-length skirt. This rare slice of pre-war chic will take some living up to, but the lucky person who can carry it off had better be prepared to start signing autographs.

Music lovers, DJs and die-hard collectors all find much to covet in Camden and in Islington's Essex Road. Bands meanwhile can record some authentic rockin' sounds of their own at a unique 50s home-studio in Muswell Hill.

CAMDEN

Sharing a name with Dobie Gray's legendary foot-stomper, you'd expect Out On the Floor to be a good source of soul, and it doesn't disappoint. On the counter are boxes of seven-inchers from the 1960s and 1970s all arranged by label (Stax, Atco, JayBoy) and watched over by a selection showcased on the wall. DJs, collectors and just plain music-lovers are alerted to the pleasures of the more obscure tunes by helpful comments written on the sleeves: 'wild boogaloo', 'killer Philly groove', or even 'wicked hustlin' instrumental'. If you are in any doubt, there are decks and 'phones for test-driving any vinyl in the shop.

Out On the Floor

Address: 10 Inverness Street, NW1
Hours: Daily 10:00–18:00
Telephone: 020 7267 5989
Web: www.geocities.com outonthefloorrecords
Tube/rail: Camden Town
Bus: 24, 27, 31, 168

Classic soul is only part of the total stock, which is equally well known for its superb selection of reggae. Original Jamaican releases fetch big money these days, and Out On The Floor prides itself on tracking down gems by major artists or on collectable labels such as Pama. Other genres that are making their presence felt are classic rock (from Led Zep to Nirvana) and even folk, which in a quiet, tankard-supping sort of way is enjoying quite a revival.

The shop is run by two extremely amiable guys called – and I'm not making this up – Mick and Finn. They've just added to their wares a range of limited-edition, four-colour silk-screen prints, including a fab portrait of Bowie and a reproduction poster for James Brown at the Apollo. These are excellent quality, and a snip at £20 each.

Get your kicks at 'Out On the Floor', just one of the essential record stores in Camden's Inverness Street

More are planned, in co-operation with friends at Delta of Venus. Without wanting to put a dampener on things, let's not forget that Camden has lost some great record shops in recent years – notably Rock On and Shakedown – so it's a matter of national significance that we all get up there and support the ones that are left.

Camden's Inverness Street has character to spare. As well as its busy market, there are cafés, comic shops and the famous pub 'The Good Mixer', one-time centre of the short-lived Britpop universe. Carry on past the pub, and past the junction where the soup kitchen still comes twice a week, and the far end of the road has one last treat in store: tucked away though it is, Sounds That Swing has for nearly a decade been flying the flag for the best in 1950s to 1970s music, drawing a steady stream of clued-up rockabillies, beat fanatics and garage punkers from far and wide.

Sounds That Swing

Address: 46 Inverness St, NW1
Hours: Wed-Sun 12:00-18:00
Telephone: 020 7267 4682
Tube/rail: Camden Town
Bus: 24, 27, 31, 168

The stock is a varied mix of CDs and vinyl, including stacks of reasonably priced reissues, as well as sought-after originals. The boxes of seven-inchers on the counter offer doo-wop, hot jivers, and new releases by modern rockin' bands. Connoisseurs and scene DJs head straight for the rare stuff, where a fistful of notes will secure hard-to-find 45s by the likes of Andre Williams or Ronny Wade. Meanwhile the main body of the shop is given over to vintage-style racks chock full of everything from blues, vocal groups and R&B, to Western swing, psychedelia and surf. As for trends, recent years have seen a big increase in demand for Detroit rock, with White Stripes fans coming in search of influential classics by The Stooges and MC5. And for regulars at the nearby Dirty Water Club (the Stripes' London club of choice!) this is also the perfect place to pick up a copy of just about anything played by the resident DJs.

When owner Barney Koumis isn't minding the shop, he's busy with his *No Hit* record label, or else helping to organize the world's hottest music festival, Viva Las Vegas (aka Heaven on Earth). You can book here for the three-night rock'n'roll extravaganza that has become a major fixture on the Vegas calendar since it started in 1998. Today's leading rockabilly acts share the stage with 1950s legends such as Wanda Jackson or Sonny Burgess, whilst top dealers from all over the US (and beyond) bring along an amazing assortment of vintage clothes. The accompanying car show, organized by SoCal's top rodders The Shifters, last year attracted 10,000 people on its own. In short, Sounds That Swing is a sure-fire winner for anyone who knows what real music is, or has a mind to find out. Time your visit right and you might even get some free soup down the road…

ISLINGTON

T he inside of Flashback may be familiar from television: it was the setting for that KFC advertisement with the soul brothers whose idea of 'working' in a record shop was to lock the door, crank up the volume, and boogie. In real life I'm glad to report you'll find the doors wide open, and owner Mark Burgess ready to deal with your most pressing musical needs (though I'm sure he knows how to cut a rug when he wants to).

The ground floor is given over to a huge stock of second-hand CDs, covering all genres and periods from blues and rock'n'roll to prog rock, exotica, psych, soul, jazz, lounge and punk. Prices range from around three to eight pounds, and as if that's not temptation enough, there's also a basement room known as 'Vinyl Heaven'. This subterranean stash of shellac keeps punters happily riffling through the racks for hours (even when they're supposed to be on their lunch break). The walls are brightened by selected gems, from original copies of Zappa's *Freak Out* to quirkier numbers such as *Enter the Dragon* (the soundtrack) or *The Doughnut in Granny's Greenhouse* by the Bonzos (all around £30–£50 each). Mark takes particular care with his grading, so that 'mint' really means what it says, and everything else gets the billing it deserves. The sleeves also get a separate grading of their own, which is especially appreciated by mail-order buyers and helps explain the success of Flashback's very active web site.

The shop caters to an impressively diverse mix of customers. Locals pop in for a bargain or to see what's new, whilst serious collectors come from far and wide in search of, say, a Jimi Hendrix Fan Club-only release, or a super rare album by Johnny Nash. Younger buyers seem to have a taste right now for 1980s US Indie and punk (bands like Huska Du, Minute Men and Big Black), whilst at the other end of the spectrum there's the old gent who drops by regularly to stock up on Dickie Valentine. Trend spotters take note: the great crooner revival might be starting right here.

Flashback

Address: 50 Essex Rd, N1
Hours: Mon–Sat 10:00–19:00,
Sun 12:00–18:00
Telephone: 020 7354 9356
Web: www.flashback.co.uk
Tube/rail: Essex Rd/Angel
Bus: 38, 56, 73, 341, 476

You'll be lucky to get out of this place alive – we're not just talking temptation here, we're talking *survival*. If you make it past the stacks of albums on the floor and the singles heaped up in boxes, you might just reach the rare stuff near the counter. But by then you'll be beyond hope. You'll have that glazed look in your eyes which says, 'I don't need food, or a car, or a house. What I really need is *that*' – pointing to some impossibly rare James Brown LP, or a signed copy of *Never Mind the Bollocks*.

Haggle Vinyl

Address: 114-116 Essex Rd, N1
Hours: Mon-Sun 09:00-19:00
Telephone: 020 7704 3101
Web: www.hagglevinyl.com
Tube/rail: Essex Rd/Angel
Bus: 38, 56, 73, 341, 476

Owner Lynn Alexander surveys all from his fortress-like counter. Around him is an estimated total of 60,000 vinyl records. Pricing is simple: 'On the floor, it's £2–3: in the racks it's £6 and upwards'. The huge range covers 'everything except classical', which in practice means rock'n'roll, jazz, easy, pop, psych, garage, funk, Krautrock, soul and even hip-hop. Reggae is a particular strength, with classic late 1970s cuts now commanding high prices from collectors worldwide (an order had just arrived from Tahiti!). LP covers brighten the walls and pose yet more threat to our chequebooks. Most eye-catching of all are 1960s classics such as Manfred Mann's *Up the Junction*, The Incredible String Band, and Love's *Four Sail* (£25–£40).

In five years Lynn has built up an amazing stock, and a following of hopelessly addicted vinyl junkies. A week here is barely enough to scratch the surface.

MUSWELL HILL

As the saying goes, 'if you want something done, ask a busy man', and Jose Espinosa is certainly one very busy man. Jose is the formidable bass player for rockabilly outfit The Cordwood Draggers, and the sole owner and operator of the unique Sisterbelle Studios. All this and a day job too!

Sisterbelle Studios

Address: Methuen Pk, Muswell Hill, N10
Hours: Phone first
Telephone: 020 8444 3471
Web: www.sisterbelle.com
Tube/rail: Alexandra Palace
Bus: 144, 299, W3, W7

By focusing on recreating a specifically 1950s sound, Jose's set-up in Muswell Hill nicely complements London's only other fully analogue suite, over at the legendary Toe Rag. For more than ten years he's been accumulating the historic gems that enable him to achieve authentic results, and he now has a superb collection. Vintage mics include the evocative RCA 77DX, also known as the Johnny Carson mic and starring in lots of black-and-white shots of the young Elvis. There's also the 44BX, designed in the late 1940s and appearing here complete with original NBC flag, as well as real rarities such as the Altec 639 Birdcage model, used specifically for recording double bass and put to work doing just that in no less a studio than Sun. Wow! Other equipment is equally impressive, especially the tube-based 'VariMu' compressor, and the late 1950s Ampex mixer. Even the reel-to-reel is an awesome mono-valve monster by Studer weighing in at nearly 200lb.

Given the emphasis on 1950s equipment, it follows that bands looking to record at Sisterbelle should be making an appropriate noise. Later styles from the 1960s onwards just won't be an ideal match, but anyone turning out hot rockin' sounds or perhaps some Western swing, blues or old-school country, would all come up a treat. The thing to do is book a trial session and see how it goes. Musicians looking to put together a CD's worth of material could spend anything from a few hundred pounds to a grand or more, at the end of which Jose can assemble a nifty package for taking off to record companies. (He's been an art director too, so the designs are really neat!) Sisterbelle also has close ties with fast-growing 1950s-scene label El Toro, that has put out an impressive series of CD and vinyl releases over the last few years and now has a major distribution deal to boot. And if bands are looking for a rockabilly DJ to warm up their next gig, then they have the ideal choice in Jose's partner, Tracy Dick. She was a regular on the Californian circuit for years, and is now helping to keep the Big Beat alive in London. A vintage studio *and* a resident DJ: now that's what I call the perfect home!

Slap that bass!

Cricklewood's 'Lifestyle Classic' is a rare source of affordably priced American autos, from 'stockers' to Hot Rods. Ton-up types and scooter fans meanwhile take their vintage machines to be spruced up in Camden..

CAMDEN

For those who already own a classic two-wheeler, Victory is a very special place. Rex and Noo will turn their hands to repairing, respraying and generally restoring to health just about any kind of pre-1980 motorcycle. For bikes this means not only British legends but older Japanese and European models too, whilst scooterists can be equally confident that their rides are in expert hands. Among recent major projects was a rare Velocette Venom Thruxton which had spent

Victory Motorcycles

Address: The Arches (down cobbled alleyway), 49 Kentish Town Rd, NW1
Hours: Tues-Sun 09.30-18.30
Telephone: 020 7284 2074
Web: www.vivienofholloway.com
Tube/Rail: Camden Town
Bus: 88

PUT A TIGER IN YOUR TANK

A 1960s Esso advertisement

most of the last 40 years lying in a garden. For sheer longevity, however, the top prize goes to Rex's own runabout, which is a beautiful 1925 Scott. Adding colour upstairs is 50s stylist 'Vivien of Holloway', long familiar on the rock'n'roll scene for her sharp repro clothing. This includes halter-neck tops and women's 'swing' trousers as well as whole rails of bowling shirts, many with leopardskin panels or saucy 'toons by Vince Ray.

80 years old and still going strong, this rare 'Scott' is a testament to the skills of Victory Motorcycles

CRICKLEWOOD

Lifestyle Classic Automobiles

Address: 16 Cricklewood Broadway, NW2
Hours: By appointment between 11:00–19:00, Mon-Sat
Telephone: 020 8450 4553
Web: www.uscc.co.uk
Tube/rail: Cricklewood
Bus: 16, 32, 189, 316

As the name suggests, this business is as much concerned with how we live as what we drive. In fact for owner Elo, the two things are inseparable. To opt for a classic auto is to make a stand against the forces of convention, which is pretty much Elo's whole *raison d'être*. From his choice of clothes to his self-designed house, everything about him is a way of announcing 'this is *me* (and I'm not like you)'. Which isn't to say he's unwelcoming – far from it! Come here to arrange a test drive, and you could stay chatting all day. But somehow I suspect that if *everyone* started queuing up to buy Vintage American Tin then he'd start selling bicycles instead.

The cars themselves are something else. The tiny showroom on Cricklewood Road can only accommodate two or three, though a lock-up a few doors down

The Lincoln 'JFK' Continental

holds a half dozen or so more. In total Elo has around 40 cars in stock at any one time, most of them dating from the 1950s to the 1970s. Earlier vehicles do occasionally join the ranks, but Elo is no great fan of their mechanics. His personal taste is for 1950s styling, 1960s technology and 1970s muscle, all of which are represented in his selection of unusual and exciting machines. King of the beasts is the 1963 Lincoln Continental, the first and — until very recently — *only* four-door convertible, with a roof

This lowrider is as radical inside as out

that folds silently into the boot at the touch of a button. Apart from its advanced electrics and prodigious fuel consumption (the engine is 7.6 litres) the model is famed above all for being the very type in which JFK was riding on that fateful day. Popular with film companies and photo-shoots, the car can be driven away for a mere £24,000 – though something tells me that Elo would not exactly mind if it sat around for a while yet.

Other vehicles typically sell for a lot less: recently these have included a 1951 Chevy 'Style Line' two-door sedan; a gorgeous 1954 Buick Special; and from the same year a Chrysler 'Windsor Deluxe', all for well under £10,000. Real standouts of late have been the customized 1941 Plymouth, and even a Ford Model T Hot Rod complete with flames painted down the sides. As an added extra, most of the cars are sourced from the mid-West US, where rust is virtually unheard of. If you can't make it to Cricklewood, then look out for Elo at one of the Ace Café Hot Rod nights, where he often puts in an appearance in an easily identifiable 'Lifestyle Classic'.

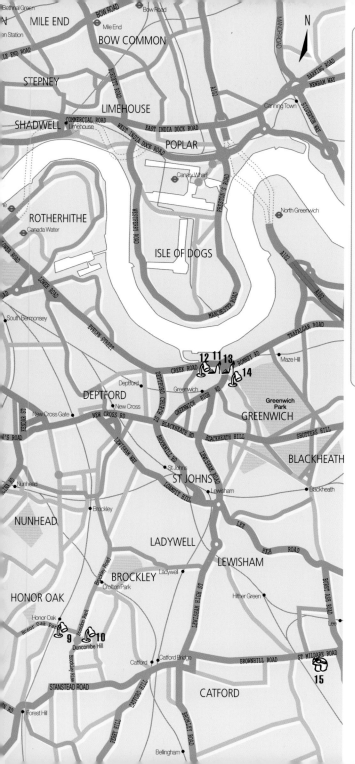

BOW COMMON

BOW ROAD

Bow Road

Mile End

STEPNEY

LIMEHOUSE

SHADWELL

COMMERCIAL ROAD

Limehouse

EAST INDIA DOCK ROAD

WEST INDIA DOCK ROAD

POPLAR

Canary Wharf

North Greenwich

ROTHERHITHE

Canada Water

ISLE OF DOGS

South Bermondsey

Nunhead

NUNHEAD

New Cross Gate

DEPTFORD

Deptford

New Cross

NEW CROSS RD

Greenwich

GREENWICH

Greenwich Park

St Johns

ST JOHNS

BLACKHEATH

BLACKHEATH HILL

SHOOTERS HILL

Blackheath

Brockley

Lewisham

LADYWELL

Ladywell

LEWISHAM

Hither Green

BROCKLEY

Crofton Park

Lee

HONOR OAK

Honor Oak

Honor Oak Park

9

10

Duncombe Hill

Catford

Catford Bridge

BROWNHILL ROAD

ST MILDARE ROAD

15

STANSTEAD ROAD

CATFORD

Forest Hill

Bellingham

1. Radio Days
2. What the Butler Wore
3. Scooterworks
4. South London Pacific
5. C.Notarianni & Sons
6. Strada Motorscooters
7. The Battersea, Vintage Fashion, Accessories & Textiles Fair
8. Inside
9. id-20th Century Design
10. Gordon Ayres, Photography
11. Emporium
12. Flying Duck
13. The Observatory
14. Twinkled
15. Ace Classics

• Railway Station

Underground Station

Docklands Light Railway

south

Choose between a 30s Italian restaurant in Battersea or a Tiki Bar in Kennington. Better still, visit both in one evening and mix the decades in style. Night owls can even enjoy an after-hours boogie to retro-friendly DJs and bands.

BATTERSEA

Notarianni has been a landmark feature in Battersea since it opened in 1936 and became at once one of the smartest and most fashionable ice-cream parlours in town. The original exterior remains to this day, and is a superb example of deco-inspired design, with 3D metallic lettering and two-tone tiling all set off very prettily by railings and flowerboxes. Some of the windows sport lovely old ads for the 'Ice Cream Alliance' dating back to the 1940s, and invoking a time when two scoops of vanilla were the typical five-year-old's delight.

C. Notarianni & Sons

Address: 142 Battersea High St, SW11
Hours: Lunch 12:00-14:45 Tues-Fri;
dinner 18:15-23:00 Mon-Sat
Telephone: 020 7228 7133
Tube/rail: Clapham Junction
Bus: 44, 49, 319, 344, 345

Incredibly, the name above the door still means exactly what it says: Notarianni's remains a family-run business, with current managers Elio and Eleanor carrying on the work of two generations before them. Diners come here first and foremost for the food, and then for the restaurant's unique ambience, which is a welcoming blend of vintage and modern design all nicely garnished with Italian family flourish. After a major refit in the 1980s the much expanded menu offers a selection of classic Italian dishes, especially pizza and pasta, though you'll still

The Deco exterior of Notarianni has been a Battersea landmark since 1936

find ice-cream as an option among the puds. The wine list is pretty serious, too, ranging from House Red at £11.50 to the rarefied taste-bud treats of Brunello and Montepulciano.

The single dining room seats 50 to 60 people, and has retained many distinctive features from its past. Chief among these is a fabulous Rock-Ola jukebox that *mater familias*, Tullia, recalls buying new in 1959 ('from Russell and Walker in Clapham' – and it cost a packet too!). Not only is this marvellous machine still in full working order and chock full of everything from Old Blue Eyes to Connie Francis, but at five plays for 20p it surely wins the prize for the best value music in London. Other retro details to look out for include the neon Visa sign, the huge 1940s wall clock, and the stylish, chrome-edged bar. There are also some fascinating photos dotted around the place, showing moments of family history.

Notarianni is a deservedly popular location with film and television companies, and for fashion shoots, too; but regulars know it best as just the kind of friendly and characterful place that draws them back again and again.

KENNINGTON

By all accounts, 'Tiki' was the name in Polynesian lore for the Great Creator, or perhaps some all-important part of him. Either way, he'd doubtless have been pretty chuffed to find himself at the centre of a craze which swept the US in the 50s. From Thor Heyerdahl's 1947 Kon-Tiki expedition to the accession of Hawaii in 1959, events for more than a decade kept attention firmly focused on the South Pacific. Popular culture was quick to take its cue, and before long a

South London Pacific

Address: 340 Kennington Rd, SE11
Hours: Thrs 18.00-24.00, Fri-Sat 18.00-02.00, Sun: phone first
Telephone: 020 7820 9189
Web: www.southlondonpacific.com
Tube/Rail: Oval / Kennington
Bus: 3, 59, 133, 159, N3, N159

zillion plastic hula girls and Easter Island heads had claimed a place in the nation's homes and hearts. The faux-exotic imagery was lurid, shameless and perfect for a decade hell-bent on having fun, and most popular of all were the Tiki Bars which sprung up in every state. Ranging in size from dinky log-cabins to the palatial excess of Ohio's legendary 'Kahiki', all offered some variation on the theme of tribal carvings, waterfalls, grass skirts and cocktails in full technicolour.

Here in drizzly England all of this passed us by. But the Tiki Bar revival of the last few years has at last brought something of the scene to our hula-starved shores. For Kennington's wonderful 'South London Pacific' we have to thank Heilco van der Ploeg, already deserving of a medal for Services to Nightlife as creator of Club Montepulciano. Partner in crime for the venue's superb South Seas styling was Josh Collins, carver of heads and retronaut extraordinaire. Together they've conjured up a temple to kitsch which deserves to be known by everyone in the land.

The bar has the atmosphere of an endless 'luau' fuelled by lethal drinks, more-ish nibbles and

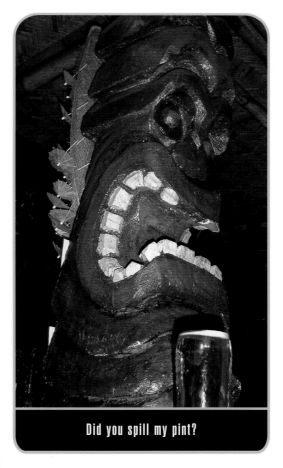

Did you spill my pint?

all manner of hep grooves from swing and blues to belly dance and beyond. Jivers get to work out at the long-running 'Hula Boogie' sessions, whilst other club nights serve up a playful mix of uptempo exotica courtesy of DJs Katmandude, Cosmic Keith, Rohan the Man and too many more to mention. At weekends there are usually live acts too, ranging from female Elvis impersonators to slick 60s popsters The Gene Drayton Unit. A late license gives 'wahines' and 'kanakas' ample time to celebrate their gods, and the occasional Sunday all-dayers welcome kids, pets, mainlanders and missionaries with equal warmth. Cheers Heilco – make mine a Zombie!

south: pad

From Clapham classics to Greenwich kitsch, South London makes a colourful contribution to the capital's design map. Honor Oak adds a stash of Panton and Pop and even takes on Hollywood with a unique photographic studio for starlets.

CLAPHAM

Inside is one of a growing number of vintage design stores to be found south of the river. By focusing on mostly Scandinavian classics, owners Georgie and Ollie offer their customers a look that is chic and modern, yet also easy to live with. The formula has proved a hit not only with dedicated style fans, but also with those coming new to mid-century furniture design.

Quality woodwork predominates, and the packed two-room shop is a symphony in oak and teak. Overcrowding is avoided by careful use of space, such as having dining chairs suspended from the picture rail (£850 for a set of six by Morgensen). Elsewhere, low-level rosewood sideboards are attended by their less familiar chest-height versions, whilst a cherry-red sofa boasts a clean-lined 1960s outline and proves very comfortable to sit on. Standouts include a superb two-tone cupboard designed in 1955 by Hans Wegner (£800), or for around the same price the striking 'Fysio' office chair by Finnish innovator, Yrjo Kukkapuro. Made from leather and bent ply, the Fysio's seat covering has also aged beautifully to a succulent, chocolate-coloured finish. Dotted here and there on surfaces are smaller items ranging from Whitefriars 'bubble glass' lamps to a set of Fiesta dishes in delightfully abstract 1950s shapes. The whole scene is doubled up in a selection of elegant French mirrors.

Prices are competitive, tending to stay below four figures, and Georgie and Ollie also pride themselves on the tip-top condition of their stock: browsers have been known to ask for catalogues, thinking everything was new.

Inside

Address: 6 Clapham High St, SW4
Hours: Tues-Sat 10:30-18:00
Telephone: 020 7622 5266
Web: www.insideoriginals.com
Tube/rail: Clapham North
Bus: 88, 155, 255, 355

Immortalise yourself in the style of Horst and Hurrell at the
Honor Oak studio of Gordon Ayres (see page 122)

GREENWICH

Flying Duck is a temple to all things kitsch. For over 15 years owners Carolyn and James have carved out their own unique space in which all the usual values simply don't apply. Instead, the beauties of Kewpie dolls and vintage board games, or of sports bags and swizzle sticks, are very much in the eyes of Flying Duck's equally varied beholders. After all, why have a run-of-the-mill lamp base when you can have one in transparent blue plastic filled with its own undersea grotto (complete with starfish)? There are many outrageous items, but there's also a solid underpinning of retro blue-chips, from Homemaker crockery to a good selection of magazines such as *Harpers*, or *House and Garden*. Larger items include lovely free-standing cocktail bars (£100–£175). Reconditioned telephones in classic designs are also very popular (£30–£75), as are the fabulous 1950s fabrics. Some of the most popular items are the vintage toys, with original Space Hoppers always in demand and the shop's most expensive item turning out to be a 1970s Chopper bike at £450.

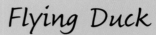

Flying Duck

Address: 320–322 Creek Rd, Greenwich, SE10
Hours: Tues–Fri 11:00-18:00, Sat/Sun 10:30–18:00
Telephone: 020 8858 1964
Tube/rail: Greenwich/Cutty Sark
Bus: 188,189

Twinkled reminds us that the 20th century's great style movements also included the inimitable '1960s Council House' school of design. As owners Kevin and Luke neatly put it: 'If it would have been in Yootha Joyce's house, then it will be at Twinkled.' In practice this means a riot of multicoloured homewares and kitchen accessories, from ashtrays, to fondue sets, board games and plastic fruit.

Twinkled

Address: The Old Petrol Station, 11-17 Stockwell St, Greenwich, SE10
Hours: Thurs/Fri 12:00-18:00, Sat/Sun 10:00-18:00
Telephone: 020 8269 0864 /07940 471569
Web: www.twinkled.net
Tube/rail: Greenwich/Cutty Sark
Bus: 177, 180, 188, 199

But all of this is only a part of the fun to be had. The emblem of the shop is the poodle, favourite of kitsch creators since the 1940s and here in a thousand guises. Elsewhere on the ground floor are furniture items ranging from G-Plan sofas and bedroom suites, to formica dining tables and a very good line in corner cocktail bars. There are also pictures by Tretchikoff, and enough 1960s and 1970s textiles to curtain the Post Office Tower. The icing on this particular fancy cake is the stunning line-up of vintage wallpaper, the result of a lifetime's avid collecting and unlikely to be bettered anywhere. Patterns include an amazing 1950s cops 'n' robbers cartoon, designs by Peter Maxx (of *Yellow Submarine* fame), and even the England 1978 World Cup Squad with a youthful Kevin Keegan. Most are sold by the roll, some are parcelled out in framed strips, and all are in strictly finite supply.

Twinkled surprises in many ways, not least by also selling a fine and characterful range of vintage clothing. The loft-like upstairs room accommodates both men's and women's items from the 1950s to the 1980s. Dead stock is plentiful, and prices are competitive, starting at around £10 for a 1980s blouse, and only rarely breaking into three figures (the record being £180 for a Jean Muir suede coat). Staff include at least one Japanese speaker at all times, and whilst enjoying a wide fan-base, the shop is hugely popular with visiting Nihonjin, both individuals and dealers. Interestingly, the Far Eastern market tends to run about 12 months ahead of trends here in the UK; on that basis, look out for a surge in demand for all things faded, time worn and decayed.

The ultimate 50s wallpaper

HONOR OAK PARK

Gordon wins a special 'One-Off Award' for bringing to this book something completely unique. I mean, who else will have you believing you're Greta Garbo or Gary Cooper? For more than ten years he's been conjuring up the kind of photographic images that hark back to the glamour days of pre-war Hollywood. The results are a spectacular re-creation of the mood, setting and sheer style found in portraits by Hurrell and Horst, or in the classic black-and-white fashion photography that graced the pages of *Vogue* from the 1930s to the 1950s.

Gordon Ayres, Photography

Address: Duncombe Hill, Honor Oak Park, near Forest Hill, SE23
Hours: By appointment
Telephone: 020 8314 1911
Tube/rail: Honor Oak Park
Bus: 122, 171

Gordon has had to learn the hard way, from studying the work of the masters and working out for himself exactly how each effect and subtle change of tone was achieved. He now commands a palette of light and shade that ranges from the hard boiled and noir-ish to the duskily romantic. A lot of Gordon's work over the years has been with the hardcore 1940s and 1950s crowd, including publicity shots for a huge number of scene bands from The Extraordinaires to Red Peters. He's even been known to set up a temporary studio at the annual Rhythm Riot weekender, where he's kept very busy by hepcats and kittens from all over the world.

For the regular shoots, clients tend to discuss in advance the image they're trying to capture, and more often than not they arrive on the day already dressed the part. The sessions take place at Gordon's sympathetically furnished Deco house, where if needs be, just about anything can be pressed into service as a prop. Rearrange the chairs, draw a couple of curtains, and the living room becomes an after-hours club; add a leather suitcase or two, and you could be in a station, waiting for the first train out of town. The only limit is your own imagination, which Gordon will gladly inspire. All he needs in return is your own fabulous self – ideally in some suitably swanky clothing.

So if you've just found your dream dress (vintage, of course) why not team it with your favourite hat and Miriam Haskell necklace, and give Gordon a ring to fix a date? To get the best results allow as much time as you can for the shoot itself – two hours minimum, and better still, half a day. For around £100 you'll get 36 studies in period-perfect black and white, and a set of standard-sized prints (rather than a contact sheet) to help you choose the ones you want enlarged. Couples, groups, all are welcome, and even a spot of location work if you've got something in mind. Genuine time travel – at a surprisingly retro price!

Since 2002, id has been brightening up the Honor Oak shopping parade with its window displays of 'Arco' lamps, Perspex sofas and assorted Pop. Owner Jerry Rossati loves the designs of the 1960s and has been hunting down mid-century classics since school. He now divides his time between 'id' and sister store C20 over in Richmond.

id – 20th Century Design

Address: 49 Honor Oak Park, SE23
Hours: Call ahead first, very flexible
Telephone: 020 8699 8087 / 07958 487654
Tube/rail: Honor Oak Park
Bus: 122, 171, P4, P12

The stock is pitched to appeal to a largely local clientèle, which means an emphasis on affordable and versatile items, rather than on radical extremes or rarities. With most things dating from the 1960s and 1970s, there's a liberal spattering of bright colours and synthetic materials, typified by Dorothea Maurer-Becher's 'Wall All' storage units. These one-piece marvels are peppered with neat little shelves and cubby-holes for stashing away any number of fiddly or easily misplaced knick-knacks.

All the usual icons are here too, notably Panton chairs in bright orange, or the same designer's 'cone' model in bottle green. There are also characterful pieces of vintage technology nestling among the leather sofas and chest-height rosewood sideboards. The Weltron 'Space Ball' radio/cassette looks rather like one of the pods from 2001, and has become a cult classic on the back of its appearance in 'Boogie Nights'.

Any idea what this is?

South of the river, vintage clothing fans head mostly for the long-established stores of Greenwich and Waterloo. But they always remember to make a date in their diaries for Battersea's regular fairs.

BATTERSEA

Launched in 2003, The Battersea Vintage Fashion Fair has already become something of an institution at the Arts Centre on Lavender Hill. Every few months the Grand Hall, with its glorious barrel-vaulted ceiling, becomes home for the day to around 100 dealers from all over the country. The clothes on offer date from the 19th century to the 1970s, and include just about every variation in neckline, waistline and hemline that the modern world can muster – not to mention all the accessories to go with them.

The fair is the brainchild of long-term vintage fans, Anita and Michelle, who set out to create a very fashion-oriented event. Their canny scheduling appeals directly to designers starting work on new collections, whilst their attention to good value caters equally for those with limited cash. Experts and newcomers alike are encouraged by the relaxed atmosphere, and when the chequebook starts to run a bit hot, there's even a chilled-out refreshment room complete with home-made cakes.

Exhibitors often save their best pieces for occasions such as this, especially

The Battersea Vintage Fashion, Accessories & Textiles Fair

Address: Battersea Arts Centre (aka The Old Town Hall), Lavender Hill, SW11
Hours: Sundays, approximately every two months, 09:30-16:30
Telephone: 020 8290 1888 (Anita & Michelle)
Web: www.vintagefashionfairs.com
Tube/rail: Clapham Junction
Bus: 77, 77A, 156, 345

A stunning 40s full-length gown takes centre stage at the
Battersea Vintage Fashion fair

when they otherwise operate from market stalls. On a recent visit, Portobello regular Vivien had brought along two corsets from the early 1800s with richly coloured silks, intricate embroidery and even a royal warrant inside – precious but eminently wearable. Likewise, Stuart Craig had marshalled a superb selection of full-length 1930s gowns, some with matching bolero jackets, all in perfect condition and a giveaway at around £200. Other standouts included Mark of Fanny Hill, with his trademark haul of Pucci's best; lace specialist Kati; Greenwich newcomers Labour of Love (with some real couture showstoppers); and André, who boasted a stash of original 1940s fashion drawings for around £150. Also turning heads were Fairweather Friends from Dorset (great 1950s dresses and evening wear); Kate O'Donnell with her well chosen printed fabrics; and Sue Coe with a whole rail of romantic Victorian nighties. Making a unique contribution meanwhile was button specialist Silvanna, with a glittering horde in bakelite, enamel and mother-of-pearl.

Anyone with even a passing interest in costume, design, jewellery or style can't fail to enjoy an event such as this. And with the fashion world forever looking to the past for inspiration, this could well be the birthplace for the next big thing. For latest information on forthcoming dates (as well as helpful directions) visit Anita and Michelle's web site: www.vintagefashionfairs.com

GREENWICH

Emporium makes an immediate impact with its snazzy window displays and well-thought-out interior. Several rooms have been knocked through into one large space and decked out with all manner of not-so-mod cons, from one-armed bandits and cocktail bars to old ads, period lights and sympathetic retro furniture.

The clothes themselves are all well zoned, and unusually offer slightly more for men than women. Nearest the door are shelves of trilbies, berets and wide-brimmed straw hats, whilst further inside are rails of suedes, leathers and fashionable combat gear. A superior collection of costume jewellery and bags

Emporium

Address: 330-332 Creek Rd, Greenwich, SE10
Hours: Tues-Sun 10:30-18:00
Telephone: 020 8305 1670
Web: www.emporiumoriginals.com
Tube/rail: Greenwich/Cutty Sark
Bus: 188, 199

Crocodile Rock in Creek Road

twinkles out from a huge display case on one wall, and directly opposite is a larger-than-average selection of evening gowns, many full length: with prices starting at just £50, these are proving increasingly popular for balls and weddings. There's also a whole rail full of little black dresses, with something for every taste, shape and occasion. Like most of the stock, these tend to be from the 1950s to the 1970s, with an occasional fast-snapped-up foray into the 1940s; and again, all are very reasonably priced at £30–£50. Emporium has also built up something of a reputation for vintage sunglasses. Those by Porsche are just about the only things in the shop likely to be priced in triple figures, but the majority sell for more like £45–£50 and include sought-after 1970s originals (all big lenses and smoked brown glass) as well as some more flamboyant numbers with diamante-encrusted frames – very Elton John!

Emporium makes a big effort to tailor its stock to the seasons, and not just to the usual extent of having more coats in winter. Summer menswear includes a wide selection of short-sleeved shirts, and for the women there's a really well chosen line-up of lightweight suits in classic 1950s and 1960s styles, cut from elegant silks or bright breezy cottons, and which can be yours for all of £30. *Wow!* Assistance is friendly and attentive (and you can ask Riley about his band, Smart Dogs, who recently played Glasto!).

Owners Jon and Jackie have been here for 18 years, and with a formula like this there's no reason why they shouldn't stay forever – reason alone to make the trip to Greenwich (though I wouldn't miss that tea-clipper).

O bservatory is a real 'finger-on-the-pulse' kind of place, as hot on contemporary street trends as the back-in-vogue fashions of yesteryear. This canny balancing act is reflected in the diversity of customers visiting the store. The younger crowd who come here for T-shirts, accessories and club gear – all new – are equally keen to snap up carefully selected vintage items

The Observatory

Address: 20 Greenwich Church St, SE10
Hours: Daily 10:30-18:00
Telephone: 020 8305 1998
Web: www.theobservatory.co.uk
Tube/rail: Greenwich/Cutty Sark
Bus: 177, 180, 188, 199

that blend seamlessly with the latest look. A good example is the trilby, once a staple of every man's wardrobe, but recently reinvented as the hip, urban female's headgear of choice (preferably worn at a jaunty angle). This is just the sort of 'everyday vintage' at which 'Observatory' excels, and it also includes Adidas sportswear, combat gear and the whole '1980s does the 1950s' thing that appeals to locals and tourists alike.

Greenwich street-style

More serious vintage aficionados are catered for in the large upstairs room that holds a classic selection of period clothing, about 70 per cent of it women's. The focus is on the 1950s to the 1970s, with occasional items from the inter-war years. A 1930s bias-cut tea dress in multi-layered chiffon (£125) competes for our attention with the 1950s A-line skirts in fashionable, strong prints, and the rails of 1960s mini-dresses. The guys meanwhile can check out a variety of 1950s suits and hats, together with a good line of Ban-Lon short-sleeved shirts.

The store also boasts the unique use of informative and characterful display boards salvaged from the V&A's famed 1995 Street Style exhibition. The head-high hoardings dotted here and there give us insights into Rude Boys or Zooties and are perfectly in keeping with the shop's fun, youthful approach. As for prices, all are very good, with very few things breaking the £50 barrier (that tea dress being a rare exception).

WATERLOO

Voted one of the '100 Best Shops in the World' (by *The Face*), every inch of this amazing shop conveys the sense of having stepped out of ordinary life into another, far more scintillating place. Once inside you're welcome to look around for as long as you like, which could easily mean a good few hours (one browser even found himself accidentally locked in at closing time!).

Radio Days

Address: 87 Lower Marsh, SE1
Hours: Mon-Sat 09:30-18:00
Telephone: 020 7928 0800
Web: www.radiodaysvintage.co.uk
Tube/rail: Waterloo
Bus: 211

Cocktail cabinets and dresses to match at Radio Days

In the first room, glassware and crockery compete for space on top of 1950s cocktail cabinets and upholstered corner bars (*very* Dean Martin), whilst compacts, perfume bottles and costume jewellery sparkle seductively from dark wood display cases. There's a huge choice of vintage magazines, from *Vogue* and *Harpers* to *Mayfair* and *Picturegoer*, along with a colourful collection of film posters, pop memorabilia and old advertising signs that decorate the walls. Nestling among the homewares and old radios are arrangements of accessories – racks of 1940s ties, hats on stands, handbags – that whet the appetite for the clothing main course in the room at the back. Stepping through, it's easy to see why this has long been a place of pilgrimage for London's latter-day vamps, bombshells, hepcats and high-rollers – in fact, for anyone in love with the golden age of glamour from the 1930s to the 1950s. There are rails of fabulous full-length gowns and cocktail dresses, along with suits, jackets, blouses, and enough pleats, peplums and sequins to fill a dressing room at MGM. Many on the swing dance scene also come here to find their wide-legged trousers and cotton dresses for a great night's hoofing at The 100 Club.

Prices are pitched at the affordable end of the spectrum: 1940s dresses range from £30–£45, ties from £15–£25, handbags average £15, brooches £10, Hawaiian shirts £30, and a set of six mid-1950s sherry glasses goes for £12.50. There are occasional one-offs that demand a higher ticket, such as the stunning 1950s dining table complete with not only six matching chairs but also a bar, cocktail cabinet and backlit wall unit – the lot for £1,500! Among other recent attention-grabbers was a seriously figure-hugging 'mermaid' dress which once belonged to the *original* Diana (Dors that is, not the Princess).

Customers include frankly everyone, from designers, film wardrobes and fashion students, to party-goers, teenagers, tourists and too many famous names to mention. Come for the full retro experience – but don't forget your sleeping bag!

Butler is a bright, funky shop, with a lovely individual feel to it — like stepping into someone's personal wardrobe. Keeping watch over the rails of well-chosen clothes are guiding spirits Paul Weller and Rita Tushingham, nicely hand painted, and underlining a house style that is very British, very streetwise and utterly unpretentious. On top of which, this is probably the only vintage clothing store with a reggae oldies specialist in the basement:

What the Butler Wore

Address: 132 Lower Marsh, SE1
Hours: Mon-Sat 10:30-18:00
Telephone: 020 7261 1353
Tube/Rail: Waterloo
Bus: 211

let the throbbing bass massage the soles of your feet whilst you check out the hats (it could catch on!)

Owners Vicki, Carla and Bridget have been at the current site for over six years, and each brings her own taste and flair to the shop's eclectic mix. Everything is hand-picked, and reproductions are studiously avoided in favour of originals. There are sometimes pieces from as far back as the 1940s, such as a waisted jacket for £75 – beautifully tailored and very *Brief Encounter* – whilst there's a decent showing from the 1950s and a huge turnout from the 1960s and 1970s. Even the 1980s have their vintage fans these days, as younger customers snap up flared skirts, ankle boots and stilettos, much to the amazement (or envy) of their mums. Shoes are a strong point all round, and include beautiful black satin heels by Rayne, as

Spot-on 60s styling at Butler

well as 1960s flatties in pink leather, all selling for between £20 and £50 (tops).

Many customers come in search of something to add a bit of character to their everyday wear, whether it's a patterned shirt, a stylish bag or a stunning leopardskin coat. But the shop is popular with purists too, especially from the 1960s scene. From time to time there are Biba dresses or real rarities such as a Mary Quant white plastic cape, and at any time you can be sure of picking up just the thing for a night out at *Mousetrap* or a Mod weekender. The menswear also scores highly with a big selection of ties, shirts, leather jackets and coats (£20–£40). Anyone looking to re-make *Up The Junction* could quite easily kit out the entire cast.

south: wheels

Southern scooterists are spoilt for choice in Battersea and Waterloo, whilst bikers are kept in clover with a world class store in Lee. Those who favour a four-wheeled ride get to gasp at the Big Yank Tin assembled in Redhill.

BATTERSEA

Since 2003, London's vintage scooter enthusiasts have had a new marker on their map, for Battersea's stylish Strada. The shop is a single-room showcase for classic and carefully selected two-wheelers, mostly of the Vespa variety, but with the occasional Lambretta showing up for the ride.

At any one time there are usually around eight vehicles in stock, and owner John McCarter is always on hand to help with the tricky task of choosing between them. Of the latest crop, a gorgeous gleaming yellow number really catches the eye, and its fact sheet tells me it's a 1966 Vespa 125 Nuova. Not only is this model increasingly rare (it was only in production for 10 months), but this particular example turns out to boast several veteran Vespa club awards to its name – and all of this for an on-the-road price of just £1850.

With a brand new Vespa Gran Turismo selling for around £2600, the comparison between vintage and contemporary scooters is one that John is very keen to make. The older vehicles are not only design icons, but actually work out cheaper to buy and more economical to run. Even a beauty like the 1960 125 sells for an undemanding £2400, and it has been fully stripped and rebuilt with the finest quality parts. As a classic vehicle it is road-tax exempt, and insurance is a bargain, too. On top of which, a collectors' item like this suffers none of the

Strada Motorscooters

Address: 167 Battersea Park Rd, SW8
Hours: Tues–Sat 10:00v18:00
Telephone: 020 7622 5588
Web: www.stradamotorscooters.com
Tube/rail: Battersea Park/Queenstown Rd
Bus: 44, 156, 344

The awesome Triumph Bonneville leads the pack at Ace Classics
(see next page)

Two-wheeled chic at Strada ◦

depreciation that afflicts a new machine. One other difference to bear in mind is that, unlike today's 'twist and go' models, the older scooters all have gears. But fears that this might make them a more difficult ride are entirely unfounded: the gears are easy to use and only add to the fun.

Strada attracts long-term scooterists, and also a growing number of newcomers, including many teenagers who have consciously chosen to buy vintage rather than new. The shop carries a full range of helmets and waterproof jackets, together with a few choice volumes for Vespa lovers' bedside reading. Who's for a rally to Brighton?

LEE

The golden age of British biking? *I was there*. OK, so I was about two years old and tucked up in a side-car, but that's not the point. Nortons, Ariels, Panthers, Vincents, I've been on them all – and the undisputed leader of the pack was the fittingly named Triumph. Ask yourself what Brando was riding in *The Wild One*: not some shiny stateside number, but a mean and dirty Triumph Thunderbird. Or take a look at the cover of Dylan's *Highway 61 Revisited*: there's that name again, emblazoned on his T-shirt. The truth is, long before anyone had heard of Yamaha or Kawasaki, this British world-beater was the very symbol of two-wheeled prowess.

Ace Classics

Address: 101-103 St Mildred's Rd, Lee, SE12
Hours: Tues-Sat 09:00-18:00 (often later midweek)
Telephone: 020 8698 4273
Web: www.aceclassics.co.uk
Tube/rail: Lee/Hither Green
Bus: 160, 202

The vintage machines are now more highly prized than ever, and one of the best places to kick-start a collection of your own is London's 'Ace Classics'. Situated beside the busy A205 in Hither Green, the shop is no museum, but more the kind of place where bike lovers come to talk twin carbs and overhead cams against a reassuring backdrop of oil and wingnuts. Of the treasures on offer, none are more sought after than the T120 Bonneville, named after the famous salt flats where Johnny Allen set a world motorcycle speed record using a Triumph engine. The Bonneville enjoyed huge success, winning races at Daytona and The Isle of Man, and a top notch 1959 original will set you back at least £10,000. Early 1960s models come up cheaper – but not much!

Father and son, Cliff and Kevin Rushworth, have seen prices rise steadily over the 15 years or so they've been in the business, and good quality vehicles are getting rarer all the time. But at the more affordable end of the spectrum you can still pick up a classic for less than £4,000. Also bear in mind that the bikes at Ace have all been fully reconditioned in the workshops at the back: the process is painstaking, and the paint jobs on the tanks are especially impressive. Many of the spares are made by Ace themselves, who are now the world's leading parts' suppliers for 1954–62 Triumphs. The range is always expanding – from petrol caps and sumps to side stands and footrests – and is already large enough to build virtually a whole bike from scratch.

From time to time an exotic guest brand pitches up in the showroom. It might be a 250cc BSA or a lovely old Ariel (around £3,000), and the chances are it'll end up in the hands of an avid collector. With shipments regularly heading off to Japan, the USA and Australia, Ace can boast a customer-base that is truly global. But they're always keen to welcome a newcomer: start with something for everyday use, and it won't be long before you're back to drool over 'sports twins' and 'café racers'.

REDHILL

Though it is now based in Surrey, Dreamcars' many years as a Battersea landmark earn it an honorary place in this book; besides which, the stock is far too good to miss.

American cars of the 1950s were always about so much more than getting from A to B: theirs is a tale of excess and excitement, and design extremes that – for a brief period – actually made the leap from drawing-board dream to production-line reality. Nowadays these great beasts are

Dreamcars

Address: 82 Holmethorpe Ave, Holmethorpe Industrial Estate, Redhill, Surrey
Hours: Mon-Fri 10:00-18:00, Sat 10:00-17:00
Telephone: 01737 765050
Web: www.dreamcars.co.uk
Tube/rail: Redhill

50s 'lipstick' tail lights

becoming ever harder to find. Fortunately owners Stuart and Milton are always dashing off to sunnier spots to find new stock, and at any one time Dreamcars has around 40 to 50 vehicles to choose from. Surprisingly, a chrome-assisted classic in good condition can be yours for as little as £8,000–£12,000 (on the road).

Whilst the emphasis is on the rock'n'roll era, there are more recent rides too, along with occasional pre-war models. Most popular are the Cadillacs and Mustangs, with souped-up 'muscle' cars enjoying a definite revival of late. Meanwhile Ford Fairlanes, T-Birds and Chevy Bel-Airs all catch the eye, as do some big-ticket exclusives. Take the 1956 Hessen Eisenhart custom wagon, which, with no fewer than eight seats, can claim to be the first ever people-mover. This half-timbered monster may not win any prizes for glamour, but as one of only two roadworthy examples in the world, it's one hell of a rarity. Or there's the super-stylish 1959 Eldorado Biarritz, one of only 99 made with 'bucket' seats (rather than the usual bench type), and with all mod cons such as air-conditioning and power brakes. In fact, the technology of the time was pushed to the limits every bit as much as the design. My favourite bit of vintage tech is the Autronic Eye, which can be found sitting on top of many Dreamcars dashboards. A popular 1950s add-on, it consists of a sensor that reacts to oncoming headlights by automatically causing its own to dip – and it still isn't standard more than four decades later!

If you're thinking of buying, then Milton's advice is first to find out all you can about the car you have in mind; time spent on research is priceless when it comes to owning a vintage auto. And besides, there's no rush. Come and enjoy a look around, arrange a test drive, or pitch up for the last Saturday of the month, when visitors are encouraged to bring along their own classic vehicles and the showroom takes on more the feel of a club meet. Either way, once you return to the world of modern motoring you'll find yourself asking: Where did it all go wrong?

WATERLOO

To get to Italy from Waterloo, no need to take the Eurostar and change in France: instead, just take a stroll down to Lower Marsh and step into Scooterworks, where you'll be instantly transported to La Bella Patria.

Owner Craig has been in the business for a decade, and opened this hugely characterful shop in 2000. The vehicles in stock are all vintage, mostly from the 1960s and late 1950s, and about 80 per cent of them are Vespas, the rest being Lambrettas. Models arrive here from the separate workshop near Tower Bridge, so if you don't see exactly what you're after, just ask what's in the pipeline. On-the-road prices tend to be around £800–£1,500, which makes these design classics irresistibly affordable. The super-rare stuff Craig is mostly happy to leave to someone else, though among his recent favourites in the shop was a very desirable 1957 Vespa 125 'low light', complete with chrome handlebars, aluminium side panels and distinctive mudguard-level lights (hence the name). This is the very model immortalized in *Roman Holiday* and is a steal at £2,000.

Scooter enthusiasts come from far and wide to bag a long-cherished model, pick up an accessory, or perhaps simply enjoy a caffeine-fuelled chat in the café at the back. Hot drinks come from a superb vintage 'Faema' on the counter. Craig restores and supplies these lovely machines, but at around £1,500 each, they're probably heading for only the swankiest coffee bars and restaurants – unless you take your coffee *very* seriously at home.

Scooterworks

Address: 132 Lower Marsh, SE1
Hours: Mon–Sat 10:00–18:00
Telephone: 020 7620 1421
Web: www.scooterworks-uk.com
Tube/rail: Waterloo
Bus: 211

Vintage vespa

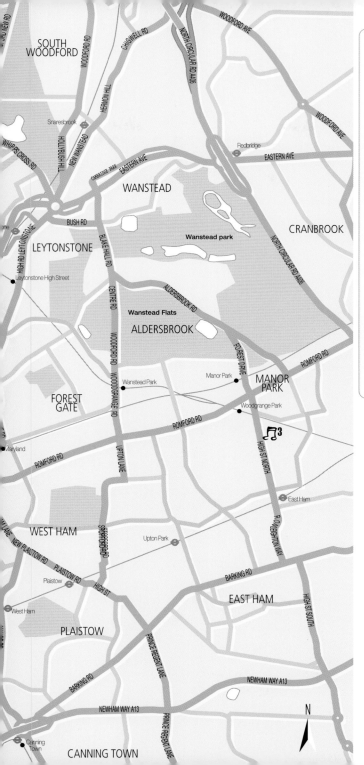

1. Supreme Drums
2. Toe Rag Studios
3. The Elvis Shop
4. Atomic Antiques
5. One Three Six
6. Two Columbia Road
7. Glitterati
8. Marcos & Trump
9. Salon
10. E. Pellicci
11. The Pleasure Unit
12. The Shop
13. Beyond Retro
14. Over Dose on Design
15. Absolute Vintage
16. Bohemia
17. Life Style
18. Story
19. Scooter Emporium

● Railway Station
◉ Underground Station
■ Docklands Light Railway

London's cafes come no finer than Bethnal Green's *E. Pellicci*, which boasts 60s decor and an equally classic East End welcome. Just up the road is a characterful nightclub with an enlightened all-eras playlist.

BETHNAL GREEN

Forget Claridge's or The Ivy: London's top table is right here in Bethnal Green Road. Locals and discerning visitors have been flocking to this sublime café since it served up its first pie and a cuppa over 100 years ago. In a street long since given over to soulless fast-food joints it now stands out more than ever as a bastion of good taste, and of those timeless virtues that are all too often called 'old-fashioned'.

E. Pellicci

Address: 332 Bethnal Green Rd, E2
Hours: Mon-Sat 06:30-17:00
Telephone: 020 7739 4873
Tube/rail: Bethnal Green
Bus: 8, 388, D3

The café has retained its period features to marvellous effect, and appears today exactly as it was when refurbished in 1960. Standing guard outside are two little trees in tubs, which frame the double doors and complement the smart, understated exterior. The name itself is announced in gleaming metallic letters, whilst a neon sign in obligatory green and red looks particularly inviting in dark winter months. Inside, the single dining room boasts wood-panelled walls that radiate warmth and welcome whilst also sporting lovely designs picked out in light and dark strips. This remarkable attention to detail is carried through to the stained-glass panels in the kitchen door and beneath the serving hatch (don't miss!), making this as perfect a post-war interior as can still be found in any restaurant in London. Long may it be preserved!

But Pellicci's unique ambience is as much a product of its customers and staff as of the way it looks. Whatever the time of day, there is an irresistible home-from-home atmosphere of a type that all those Seattle Coffee Factories can only dream of. Over plates of mash and mugs of tea, diners of all ages and every combination

From its neon sign to its original 60s interior, E. Pellicci is every inch a classic

of race and creed keep up a kind of jovial open-forum that is further enlivened by Signor Pellicci himself, still going strong after more than 40 years at the helm. The marriage of Latin enthusiasm and Old East End vitality seems as natural as it is compelling, and anyone feeling the least bit down should simply hot foot it over here to put the world in a far happier light.

Last but not least there's the food, which concentrates on much loved hardy annuals such as bacon sarnies and home-made pies. Ciabatta rolls add a relatively modern touch, whilst the cakes and crumbles are guaranteed to bring on a warm

Mod faves The Impact turn it up at The Pleasure Unit

glow. The all-day menu is as suited to early shift workers tucking into roast chicken at 10.00am as it is to students enjoying breakfast at noon. Meat and two veg for under a fiver: boot-filling obligatory!

East End music lovers have a gem on their hands in the funky, fiercely individual 'Pleasure Unit' on Bethnal Green Road. The outside gives little away, though the faintly psychedelic lettering is a clue. Inside, the 1960s theme comes to the fore, with guiding spirits The Who and other 'faces' on the walls and a vintage scooter in the corner emblazoned with the venue's logo.

The Pleasure Unit

Address: 359 Bethnal Green Rd, E2
Hours: Sun-Thurs 18:00-24:00,
Fri/Sat 18:00-02:00
Telephone: 020 7729 0167
Web: www.pleasureunitbar.com
Tube/rail: Bethnal Green
Bus: 8, 388, D3

The place is more cosy than cavernous, and its pillars and wooden floor give it the feel of a bite-sized Dingwalls. Most important of all is the music policy of owner Nigerian Nick, who oversees a string of separate club nights unified only by their quirky eclecticism and commitment to good honest fun. Retro sounds are not the only ones to get an airing here, but they do form something of a backbone. Among the regular tenants of late have been the Lunar Lounge crew, dishing up a blend of 'Hammond grooves, exotica, latin boogaloo, sleazy-listening, sitar beat and Japanese club pop'. They always offer a live act too, with bands ranging from film-theme aficionados The Adventures of Parsley to the swinging evangelism of Reverend Cleatus and the Soul Saviours. And talking of soul, monthly night 'Shake' offers yet more proof of the great Northern revival. Guest DJs from London's top soul clubs dust off their rare 45s, and for six free-admission hours bring a little bit of Wigan to E2. Other fixtures on the calendar have included Mod-fest 'Hipsters', for a clued-up, dressed-up crowd, and 'Hands Off She's Mine', a popular 'anything goes' event where Daft Punk meets Elvis in a Prince Buster style!

Lurking in this mix are some familiar faces wearing their occasional DJ hats: Caspar from Portobello market's Dandy in Aspic; and from Toe Rag Studios the analogue Svengali Liam Watson. Add it all up, and you have the kind of adult party-room that every neighbourhood could do with. There are even night buses running right outside, which is great news for those who can't afford to live nearby but have to slum it up West instead.

east: pad

The specialists of Shoreditch and Bethnal Green have supplied many a design gem to local lofts and bars, not to mention connoisseurs the world over. But London's fastest-changing area has its downside too: best to call ahead to avoid turning up at a building site!

BETHNAL GREEN

For getting to see a huge variety of vintage furniture and lighting in the course of one short walk, the East End has to be one of the best areas in London. And an integral part of the E1 design trail is Atomic Antiques, which opened in Shoreditch High Street in 2001. Owner William Simms has filled the shop with mostly post-war items, displaying a particular fondness for high quality, natural materials.

Atomic Antiques

Address: 125 Shoreditch High St, E1
Hours: Sat/Sun 11:30-17:30, weekdays call to confirm
Telephone: 020 7739 5923 / 07946 289878
Tube/rail: Old Street/Shoreditch
Bus: 26, 35, 47, 67, 78, 149, 242

It's no surprise to find the Scandinavians here in force, especially when it comes to chairs. Hans Wegner's famed 'Sawback' design dates from the late 1940s, and its trademark A-shaped legs can be yours for around £850. At the cheaper end of the scale are originally mass-produced but now highly collectable pieces such as Wegner's stackable, teak-veneered, three-legged numbers, or the iconic 'Ant' chairs designed by Arne Jacobsen in 1952 and bearing more than a passing resemblance to their animal namesakes (£175 each).

But the Danes are not the only ones to score with the fine woodwork. Just as outstanding in design and execution is an English dining table from the late 1950s constructed from a solid slab of elm. It has surfaces that demand to be touched, and is the kind of piece that could only have been made before British elm stocks were ravaged by disease in the 1970s. In fact, vintage furniture often incorporates materials that are not as available as they once were. The classic example is rosewood, now protected by conservation measures but also thankfully preserved

The beautiful pistillo is one of the most evocative designs of the 60s, here seen lighting up Atomic

in all the silky veneers of 1970s sideboards, and a whole host of other classic pieces going back as far as the original Eames loungers. Recycling this priceless inheritance is a key part of what Atomic sets out to do.

Chair-hunters should also look out for the swivel designs by Pierre Paulin, collapsibles by Giancarlo Piretti, and Harry Bertoia's Diamond models from 1958. There's a good selection of lighting here too – including giant-sized 'pistillos' – and some late 1960s Op Art in glass and perspex. Prices are very fair, and customers are an eclectic mix of locals, connoisseurs and intrigued passers-by.

Sandwiched between the bagel bar and the fish shop, '136' is another of Columbia Road's Sunday-only gems. Competing with all those flowers is no easy job, but the sputniks and chrome shades in the window prove an effective lure. Once inside, browsers discover a shop with hidden depths, and a pricing strategy that is geared to making sales. A real highlight is the range of Poole pottery, which draws serious collectors from far and wide. Owner Sherralyn has been a fan of the simple, classic tableware for as long as she can remember, and has amassed at '136' one of the most impressive hordes in London. Best known of the Poole line-up is probably the twin-tone series, which remains hugely popular. Its elegance, attractive colour palette and sheer affordability make it an ideal ambassador for modern ceramic design, and just the kind of thing you won't be scared to use everyday. Sherralyn also operates a matching service for those already building up a set.

Holding its own with all the fine

One Three Six

Address: 136 Columbia Rd, E2
Hours: Sun 10:00-15:30
Telephone: 020 7729 2740/07958 441312
Tube/rail: Shoreditch
Bus: 26, 48, 55

Liqueurs and Lichtenstein

crockery is a selection of furniture and decorative arts from the 1950s to the 1980s. Sideboards include a beautiful Swedish example, much longer than average, and its familiar dark wood exterior thrown into rare relief by the maple veneer inside (all for £750). Those on a limited budget can still afford the popular Scandy look, with other sideboards selling for as little as £300. It's no wonder this shop gets crowded! Coffee tables are always in demand, not least because they can be picked up and taken away, whilst glassware is by Murano, Whitefriars, Holmgaard and also Orrefors (a house favourite).

The artwork concentrates on Op and Pop by Lichtenstein and Bridget Riley, usually in modern, licensed prints. Also on the walls are original film posters, photographs and some work by up-and-coming younger artists. Add in a 'lucky cat' or two for good measure, and you have a great little business, well worth a visit.

L ike the street after which it is named, Two Columbia Road is busiest on a Sunday morning when the famous flower market draws huge crowds to the area. But unlike many of its neighbours, this shop also opens during the week, when there's rather more room to enjoy the mid-century treats on offer.

The stock is eclectic and varies enormously, depending on what has lately caught the eye of owner Keith Roberts and father Tommy, who helps with the buying. Between

Two Columbia Road

Address: 2 Columbia Rd, E2
Hours: Tues–Fri 12:00–19:00, Sat 12:00–18:00, Sun 10:00–15:00
Telephone: 020 729 9933
Web: www.twocolumbiaroad.com
Tube/rail: Old St/Shoreditch
Bus: 26, 48, 55

them they show a taste for the quirky and undervalued, coupled with a firm commitment to Scandinavian classics and British furniture design. An original Jacobsen 'Egg Chair' in brown leather makes a typical window-filler, where it might be joined by a solid rosewood desk by Finn Juhl: his name is less celebrated than some, but his work is both innovative and of very high quality, and for those reasons just the sort of thing that Keith likes to champion. Likewise the 1960s designs of Arne Vodder, whose tables and chairs further extend the Danish woodworking tradition.

Chairs enjoy a strong showing all round, and include several modern archetypes such as Harry Bertoia's Bird, Peter Chyczy's collapsible Garden Egg, the Swan, and Pierre Paulin's post-Eames ottoman set. Among the British delegates are chests of drawers by Sylvia Reed, classics by Milne and, most strikingly of all, a beautiful,

The 1947 cloud table

sitting-room-friendly Cloud Table by Neil Morris (made in 1947, and a snip at £550).

Filling in the gaps are a host of smaller items, ranging from typewriters and 1950s crockery to some Murano glass vases for displaying all those fresh flowers. For sheer entertainment value top marks go to the collection of 1970s toy robots, every one a mechanoid marvel and priced between £25 and £50 depending on size (watch out for those metal pincers!).

SHOREDITCH

W ith their stem-like single pedestals and smooth-moulded outlines, Eero Saarinen's 'Tulip' chairs were the height of 1960s dining-room chic. As bona fide icons they hold their appeal today, and are perennial bestsellers at the swish little chalet that is Bohemia, tucked inside Spitalfields market.

The snug space accommodates a surprisingly wide variety of design desirables that spill out on to the concourse around the shop itself. Quality control is high, and the very

Bohemia

Address: Gate 1, Old Spitalfields Market, E1
Hours: Wed-Fri 12:00-14:00, Sun 10:30-17:00
Telephone: 020 7375 3283
Web: www.retrotrading.co.uk
Tube/rail: Liverpool St
Bus: 67

few reproductions among the vintage pieces are all clearly labelled as such. Best of all are the prices, with nothing reaching four figures and most of the major items – including those 'Tulips' – pitched in the low hundreds.

Other seating includes classics by Bertoia and Panton, as well as less well-known finds such as the chrome-framed chair with tanned-hide sling by Charlotte Perriand. She worked with Le Corbusier, but is only now receiving the recognition she deserves, and interestingly her signature designs are almost always snapped up by Bohemia's female customers (thesis by email please!). Lighting is another real strength, and extends to such gems as a pair of 1940s Venini chandeliers in two-tone glass complete with matching wall lights. All the fittings have been rewired, and Italian post-war names predominate, though owner Polly Pollard is flexible on dates and origins, just as long as items have that priceless 'wow' factor. A

Design treasures in Spitalfields

good example is the 1950s 'Rocket Lamp' that could be purchased with Green Shield stamps at the time, but which now stands out for its real period character.

Also on offer are tile-surfaced 1960s coffee tables with ceramic sunbursts or abstract mosaics, and striking one-offs such as the 1970 Joe Colombo 'Boby' trolley in black-and-white plastic (much better than the coloured versions). Customers mix and match, rather than trying to recreate any one decade, and enjoy exploring all the combinations of shade and shape. As one of them was moved to comment: 'Now I realize how much fun my parents had!'.

Don't go looking for a big sign: if you're lucky, Life Style will announce itself by way of a crude, hand-written notice in the window. Failing that, you'll just have to watch out for the bare-bricked showroom packed with wide leather sofas and coffee tables, and presided over by larger-than-life character Stephane Raynor – MC, ringmaster and businessman extraordinaire.

Stephane has a freebooting, high-octane approach to life, which has its roots back in the King's Road of the 1970s. That's

Life Style

Address: 17 Lamb St, Old Spitalfields Market, E1
Hours: Mon-Fri 14:00-17:00, Sat/Sun 12:00-18:00
Telephone: 020 7247 503
Tube/rail: Liverpool St
Bus: 67

where he set up 'Acme Attractions', selling funky retro clobber to free spirits such as Don Letts, before moving on to his next venture, the legendary 'Boy London'. He

Close encounters of the lighting kind

kitted out punks and New Romantics, and like neighbour Malcolm McLaren, created a fashion frisson by respectfully pillaging the past. These days his thing may be Panton, not pantaloons, but the attitude remains the same – hence the throw-away, non-committal name.

Stock selection is based on instinct rather than any strict rules, and the focus might change at any time. Of late there's been a definite 1980s revival going on, with renewed demand for mirror-surfaced monochromes and stark, oriental-influenced outlines. But this is already shifting quite nicely into a more functional 1940s look, with no-nonsense shapes and traditional woods coming to the fore. Fortunately the space is large enough to accommodate a variety of styles, spread out through a suite of rooms at the rear as well as a sizeable basement area (nicknamed Low Life). Prices range from £20 to £2000, and standouts include the iconic 1970s chrome and canvas hanging chair (like a giant-sized bird cage), along with mushroom-shaped floor lamps and metallic chandeliers.

The best time to come is on a Sunday afternoon when the shop packs out and customers enjoy a vibe that Stephane sums up as 'pure rock'n'roll'.

'Champagne' chair from 1957

Proof that not every overdose is a bad thing, this Brick Lane store has for the past six years been treating its customers to an excess of classic mid-twentieth-century furniture. With glass walls on two of its sides, the bright main room resembles a huge display case, inside which the sofas, chairs and tables are so plentiful they stack up in the corners before overflowing into a smaller room downstairs. The walls – where they are still visible – sport a prestigious collection of mainly British Pop Art by the likes of Allen Jones and Peter Blake.

Over Dose on Design

Address: 182 Brick Lane, E1
Hours: Mon–Sun 11:00–18:00
Telephone: 020 7613 1266
Web: www.overdoseondesign.co.uk
Tube/rail: Shoreditch/Aldgate East
Bus: 8, 67, 388

Taking centre stage are assorted design icons including Eames' lounger and ottoman sets, as well as chairs by George Nelson (Coconut) and Verner Panton (both the Cone and Heart varieties). More often than not, superstars such as these have been made continuously under licence since they were first created, and the value of any specific example will depend as much on the time and place of its manufacture as on its general condition. Fortunately, store manager Michael has an encyclopaedic knowledge of just those little details that potential buyers might otherwise overlook. Take that famous lounger: the first thing to check for is the Eames copyright label, which is the mark of quality whatever the period. Then there's the shell – which could be rosewood, walnut or cherrywood, depending on the age – and also the cushions, which are foam-filled these days and consequently somewhat fatter and less streamlined than the feather-stuffed originals. Even the feet and the shock absorbers contain vital clues that can mean a difference in price of several thousand pounds.

With the more unusual items there's no doubting their origins. Among the standouts are the lovely and rare 'Champagne' chairs by Erwine and Estelle Laverne, dating from 1957 and embodying a pure, space-age aesthetic remarkably ahead of its time. Understated, home-grown pieces by the likes of Milne and Race also nestle among the more luxurious US designs, whilst major Danish names are lurking too, somewhat in the background. There are even some classic Bang & Olufson TVs that blend in perfectly with their surroundings. Prices start at a couple of hundred pounds for a generic glass and chrome coffee table, and frequently rise to four figures. The atmosphere in the shop is at once unpressurized, yet charged with genuine enthusiasm for the wonders of modern design.

From the glamour of Columbia Road to the bargains of Cheshire Street, the East End has retro chic to suit all tastes and budgets. The shops themselves range in size from enormous, fun-filled warehouses to exquisite boutiques.

BETHNAL GREEN

London's well-served fans of vintage costume jewellery have another treat in store at Glitterati, upstairs from Marcos & Trump. Owners Julie and George have pooled their talents to create a wonderfully eclectic mix, and one that excels in several specialist areas.

Glitterati

Address: 1st Floor, 146 Columbia Rd, E2
Hours: Sun 09:00–16:00
Telephone: 07778 045973
Tube/rail: Shoreditch
Bus: 26, 48, 55

Most remarkable – because so unusual – is the selection for men, especially the cufflinks; these date from late Victorian to the early 1970s, and the range must surely rank as one of the very best available anywhere. Many are period marvels such as the 1954 Playboy designs, or those with miniature pin-ups of Marilyn Monroe. The quality is outstanding too, with high standards of manufacture and tip-top materials. There are desirable sets with matching tie-pins, and real surprises, such as the pair that tidies away into the hinged top of a very dapper clothes' brush. To complete the look there are also ties and shirts, whilst prices offer little hindrance, starting at £15 and topping out at a little over £100 for the rarities. Customers include the suave, the debonair, retro-rockers and assorted eternal bachelors.

Julie meanwhile looks after the ladies, and a fine job she does of it, too. An avid collector all her life, she now offers a sizeable spread that majors on the key US names: Haggler, Haskell and Trifari. Also included is personal favourite Robert DeMario, and European designs by the likes of Dior and Schiaparelli. The emphasis is on wearable, less theatrical pieces, the bulk of which date from the late 1940s and early 1950s. Bracelets, stars, feathers of crystal, sprays of glass flowers, and

'Miss Crawford will take the Trifari.' Hollywood glamour at Hackney prices, thanks to Glitterati

lucite necklaces with matching ear-rings (£100), are displayed with inspirational images from the silver screen. Classic, daisy-shaped enamelled brooches are also here by the boxful, at once epitomizing 1950s design, yet also looking utterly contemporary. Add in a selection of vintage scarves to effect full transformation into a neighbourhood fashion icon, and Glitterati is quite simply a 'must' for all lovers of vintage glamour – whatever their budget.

Eclectic, going on eccentric, Marcos & Trump is an always-enjoyable shop that defies most conventional categories. Tea-sets, sherry glasses and handbags fill the tiered shelves, whilst 1960s picnic hampers and button-filled baskets are dotted around the floor. Elsewhere are lampshades, quilts, vanity cases and clocks, interspersed with sympathetic new stuff such as sequinned slippers or artificial flowers. A sense of 'tasteful kitsch' hovers over some of the items, but not such as to detract from their more blue-chip neighbours. Standouts among the artful clutter include the vintage greetings cards, many of which boast superb 1950s sci-fi images of children in rocket ships complete with their pets in doggy spacesuits (a giveaway at £4/£5 each).

The vintage clothing, meanwhile, is a joint exercise with sister shop Salon, who take much of the couture and evening wear, whilst M&T concentrates on a more fun, light-hearted but still party-perfect wardrobe of 1960s day-glo mini dresses, 1940s blouses, nighties, undies, and elegant sheaths in tangerines and pinks (typically around £50). There are always some out-and-out glamour numbers too, such

Marcos & Trump

Address: Gr Flr, 146 Columbia Rd, E2
Hours: Sun 09:00–16:00
Telephone: 07956 465126
Tube/rail: Shoreditch
Bus: 26, 48, 55

Fab 40s fabric at Salon

as a 1940s full-length black silk gown for £90 that would hold its own in any company. Budding Imeldas and Ivanas would probably buy the lot!

E very time I've been to Salon the window has showcased some rare and breathtaking dress of truly outstanding quality – and I'm talking about the kind of thing that stops traffic (or at least it does when I'm driving!). This could be a killer 1940s ball gown, or a 1950s wedding dress with scalloped tiers of lace on the bodice and calf-length full skirt – real fairytale stuff, no question.

It comes as no surprise to learn that owner Annalise is also a celebrity stylist, and her impeccable taste is as evident in the delightful feminine décor of the shop as in the clothes. The two rooms contain a very varied mix, which might include a unique 1920s opera coat in black silk with white fur collar and cuff, as well as 1950s Dior, 1940s Schiaparelli, and occasional items from as recently as the 1970s (if they're special enough). Given the quality of the stock the prices are extremely good, starting at around £200. (That amazing 1950s wedding dress was priced at a giveaway £250.)

Customers tend to be fashion-fluent, and Salon's rails reflect the latest catwalk trends. Each new season is sure to revive a style or past decade. Whichever it is, the originals will be available right here – better made and at a fraction of the cost.

Salon

Address: 142 Columbia Rd, E2
Hours: Sun 09:00–16:00
Telephone: 020 7739 2954 / 07778 045973
Tube/rail: Shoreditch
Bus: 26, 48, 55

SHOREDITCH

L ike waistlines, vintage clothing shops are definitely getting bigger. In recent years a number of warehouse-sized stores have opened, and the latest to join the club is Absolute Vintage. The high-ceilinged single room is packed with choice, but what recommends the venture most is its amazing range of women's shoes: upwards of 2000

Absolute Vintage

Address: 15 Hanbury St, E1
Hours: Tues–Sat 12:00–19:00, Sun 11:00–19:00
Telephone: 020 7247 3883
Tube/rail: Liverpool St
Bus: 67

Walk the rainbow

pairs are racked up around the walls, in a display given further impact by its being colour sorted. Looking for something in red? Then take your pick from several hundred courts, wedges, mules and slingbacks all in a variety of shades from pillar-box to crimson. Best of all is the corner where the more unusual colours are gathered together in a footwear fiesta of tangerines, turquoises and fashionable lemon yellows. Dates could be anywhere from the 1920s to the 1990s, with a good showing for post-war styles, and all priced between £5 and £65.

'Absolute' also carries a vast quantity of clothing essentials, including a section for the guys. Thus 1980s dresses and 1970s coats can be twinned with 1950s and 1960s tops and skirts, whilst all can be instantly accessorized with the shop's plentiful jewellery, bags and belts. Nice touches, in among the shelves and rails, are the mock market stalls reminding us of owner Dean's open-air background on Portobello Road. Customers are a diverse mix of students, locals, models, designers and dedicated followers of fashion. Oh yes, and people who love their shoes!

The all-new East End now adds another star to its bill in the shape of Beyond Retro, an enormous warehouse of all-American vintage clothing. The size of the operation and its location helps keep the prices tantalizingly low. Hundreds of 1960s and 1970s dresses go for an average of £10, and the same money will even

Beyond Retro

Address: 110–112 Cheshire St, E2
Hours: Daily 10:00–18:00 (Sun from 08:30)
Telephone: 020 7613 3636
Web: www.beyondretro.com
Tube/rail: Shoreditch
Bus: D3

buy a simple, super-fashionable cotton number from the 1950s. T-shirts from the 1970s and 1980s are hugely popular, and at only £4, one can see why. Also going for a song are jackets in satin or fringed suede, jeans, and a whole rail of wedding and prom dresses, many of which are snapped up for their fabrics alone.

Menswear makes up about 50 per cent of the total, and includes sought-after Western, bowling and Hawaiian shirts, as well as knits, coats, shorts, tracksuits, pegs, drainpipes, ties, and just about everything else a retro guy might need. Accessories are also here in force – shoes by the shelf-load, boots, trainers, handbags, flight bags, hats, caps and belts – along with all the street-fashion must-haves such as army fatigues and workwear: some engineer's dungarees from the early part of last century win the prize for the oldest items in stock. Younger customers, especially students, come here to pick up a bargain and for the fun of rummaging through the huge stock. But Beyond Retro also caters for those with less time (and usually bigger budgets!), and areas are set aside for carefully sorted, well displayed and slightly 'higher end' pieces that typically reflect the latest catwalk trends. Of late, the 1950s glamour items have been the ones enjoying star treatment, half-filling one room with a sensational turn-out of chiffons, tulles and appliqués, all boasting the season's hottest cuts. Even these showstoppers sell for as little as £35, rising to around £60 for a full-skirted evening gown. Depending on demand, the era or style in the spotlight might change at any moment, but manager Kate has a keen eye for fashion trends, and her showcase selection can be relied upon to deliver the goods. Irresistible, and open seven days a week!

Local commerce these days may have more to do with coffee shops than sweat shops, but clothes and furniture are still a mainstay of the many businesses now propelling the East Ends retro retail boom. Among them is the unique destination shop Story, where every one of the carefully selected items, like the building they are in, has a tale to tell.

Owners Ann and Lee (co-founder of the vintage pioneers, Flip) preside over a huge ground-floor showroom, where just about anything might form a part of the beautiful displays – just as long as it meets their exacting standards for quality and character. Clothing includes superbly structured 1950s cocktail dresses hung individually on the walls like works of art – which of course they are. A fitted jacquard coat catches the sunlight, its woven roses wavering between turquoise and sea green, whilst shawls, throws and carpets all add their own chapters to the one big 'story' in fabric. Elsewhere, handbags and exquisite vintage compacts twinkle out from corners, and glass cases frame rarer, more delicate items such as the feathered mules by Ferragamo (probably made for

Story

Address: 4 Wilkes St, E1
Hours: Daily 13:00–19:00
Telephone: 020 7377 0313
Tube/rail: Aldgate East/Liverpool St
Bus: 67

Dream dresses with furniture to match

a ballet in the 1950s). Scents, soaps and the smell of coarse string meanwhile remind us that Story sets out to leave none of our senses unexcited.

In amongst these goodies, or sometimes helping to show them off, are equally well-chosen pieces of furniture, where the emphasis is likewise less on date or provenance than on the more immediate values of texture, tone and shape. Modernist chairs with sinuous bent-ply frames make an elegant backdrop to a mix of distressed antique armoires and Mies van der Rohes. Stock is ever-changing, but is always sharp, desirable and contemporary – in a historically enriched sort of way. Don't expect rails of clothes and great heaps of sofas: Story is all about giving things their space. But what things! Come in search of a pair of shoes, and chances are you'll also leave with a table and some hand-made candles.

Now here's a veritable Shangri-La. Visits have to be timed right, as opening hours are limited, but the effort is rewarded with clothes of such high quality and so reasonably priced that you'll hardly believe it's true. The icing on the cake is proprietor Sharon who is the embodiment of charm as well as being knowledgeable and passionate

The Shop

Address: 3 Cheshire St, E2
Hours: Thurs 12:00–18:00, Sun 09:00–15:00
Tube/rail: Shoreditch/Aldgate East
Bus: 8, 67, 388

about everything she sells. No wonder that customers return again and again, and have even been know to queue outside before doors open just to be sure of getting first sight of new arrivals.

Stock is predominantly 1950s and 1960s, occasionally earlier, and the space is shared between womenswear and a lovely selection of vintage textiles. A sleeveless 1960s dress in a geometric, tapestry-effect print sells for a mere £12, whilst a stunning pink mini-dress, heavily sequinned with a ruffled neck, can be yours for an incredible £30. The same amount will even secure a Jackie O lime-green dress by Valentino, complete with cinched front and a lovely opal buckle. Meanwhile, gorgeous 1950s hats with veils, bows and flowers are generally priced at under a tenner. There's also a large selection of handbags from the 1950s to the 1970s, – and you'll be hard-pressed to find one for more than £15.

Stylish regular at The Shop

The textiles, like everything else in The Shop, are very well displayed, especially given the compact space. A wall of dark wood shelves contains a colourful stock of vintage fabrics, including tablecloths and pillow-cases as well as a fine selection of curtains. These come in a variety of bold period prints and are generally priced below £30. Stock is ever-changing, as turnover is very fast: that anything stays on the rails longer than five minutes I find amazing.

For a perfect day up East, browse the Elvis rarities in Manor Park and check out the vintage drums in Walthamstow. Finish in style by heading off to Homerton to record your next single at the all-analogue studio favoured by The White Stripes.

HOMERTON

Toe Rag Studios is a little corner of analogue heaven, carefully pieced together by owner Liam Watson. If you've heard The White Stripes' album *Elephant* then you already know what Liam and his valves can do. As the sleeve notes proudly state: 'No computers were used in the writing, recording, mixing or mastering of this record' – just sweat, genius and Toe Rag's superb vintage equipment.

Toe Rag Studios

Address: Glyn Rd, Homerton, E5
Hours: Phone to book
Telephone: 020 8985 8862
Web: www.toeragstudios.com
Tube/rail: Homerton
Bus: 236, 276, 52

Tucked away in a quiet Hackney street, and cunningly disguised as a bookbinders, the studio is a perfect time capsule with technology straight out of a classic black-and-white sci-fi movie. There are voltmeters, big-needled gauges and shiny, faintly sinister machines covered in bakelite knobs and labels such as 'Frequency Analyzer' or 'Output Attenuator'. The names of legendary manufacturers are everywhere, from Ampex and Vox to Ludwig drums (a 1965 kit) and organs by Hammond and Farfisa. But the focal point is Liam himself: engaging, enthusiastic, and utterly dedicated to what he does, he looks like the kind of swinging boffin Steed would ask for help if Mrs Peel were in trouble. (From time to time you can catch him DJ-ing too, at venues such as The Pleasure Unit.)

The studio is very much an ongoing project, the latest addition being a relatively lavish 16-track recorder with spools for two-inch tape and a generous array of dials and patch-bays to play with. The prize for the oldest piece of equipment, and the most evocative, goes to the 1956 mixing desk that came from some other wannabe

Vintage skins and a lifetime's expertise at Walthamstow's
Supreme Drums (see next page)

studio called Abbey Road. Apart from the Stripes, other bands to have worked here include cult Billy Childish outfits Thee Headcoats and The Buff Medways, along with The Blue Star Boys, Big Joe Louis, and original 1950s rocker Ronnie Dawson.

If you're itching to record some of your own no-nonsense, straight-from-the-heart rock'n'roll, then this is definitely the place for you. Give Liam a ring first to confirm current rates, and rest assured that you'll be getting a good deal, and a unique experience.

MANOR PARK

For Elvis fans, the centre of the world will always be Memphis, but the next best thing has to be our very own East Ham. In this unlikeliest of spots, the amazing Elvis Shop has been selling The King for over 20 years. The bulk of the stock is made up of several thousand CDs and considerably more LPs, singles, EPs and 78s, covering every split second of the man's recording career.

Obviously all the hits are here, but you'll also find as many out-takes and alternative versions as you can handle, along with live shows, interviews, and repackagings from every corner of the globe. On a recent visit, I was intrigued by a dinky 10" album simply entitled 'Janis & Elvis'. Janis Martin was often marketed as 'The Female Elvis' (still is!), but I'd

The Elvis Shop

Address: 400 High St North, Manor Park, E12
Hours: Mon–Sat 10.30-18.00
Telephone: 020 8552 7551
Web: www.elvisshop.demon.co.uk
Tube/Rail: East Ham / Woodgrange Park
Bus: 101, 104

The King is alive and well in Manor Park

never heard of a disc bringing the two of them together. Turns out the album was only released in South Africa, and without Colonel Parker's say-so. It was withdrawn as soon as he found out, and copies are exceedingly rare, typically fetching around £1,500.

The good news is, for us ordinary lay-worshippers there's more than enough here to be getting on with, and owner Chris is as welcoming to the novice as to the lifelong true-believer. The roll-call of customers is a kind of 'UN meets the Seven Ages of Man', with everyone paying their dues from Brazilians and Icelanders to Megadeth's guitarist and the local 10 year old escorted by his mum. One regular has even changed his name to Elvis Presley by deed poll. As well as the music there are also books, magazines, photos and posters, many of which are highly sought-after in their own right. Best to phone ahead to make sure they're open, and be prepared for an experience like no other.

WALTHAMSTOW

I f you're thinking of buying a drum kit, then why not treat yourself to a classic? Just get yourself down to Supreme Drums to talk to skins supremo, Lou Dias.

A big-name kit from the 1950s or 1960s and in good condition will typically set you back between £800 and £1200. Demand waxes and wanes, though the 'Ludwig' brand remains a perennial favourite on the back of its Beatles links. Younger buyers have picked up in the wake of Britpop, whilst the steadiest custom tends to come from jazz musicians, many of

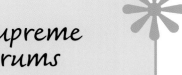

Supreme Drums

Address: 208 Forest Rd, Walthamstow, E17
Hours: Mon–Sat 11:00–17:00
Telephone: 020 8520 3873
Web: www.supremedrums.com
Tube/rail: Blackhorse Rd
Bus: 123

whom have kept faith with the same manufacturer over long performing careers. Currently in vogue are the early 1970s 'Vistalite' designs in clear Perspex, as once used by rock god John Bonham of Led Zep: a single Vistalite snare will set you back £200, and a full kit more like £1500. Back in the 1970s the done thing was to put lights inside the drums for effect, so let's hope the new owners do the same.

east: wheels

The gates of Dray Walk were built for barrel-laden carts but these days open wide for the chic two-wheelers from 'Scooter Emporium'. These mobile design classics are the perfect complement to all the nearby vintage clothing and furniture.

SHOREDITCH

Marco and Steven have run their large, airy and scooter-packed emporium off Brick Lane for the last five years, after relocating their long-established business from Essex. At any one time you'll find dozens of vintage machines to choose from, all fully reconditioned, road-going and sourced direct from Italy. Prices start at about £1000 (inclusive of tax, MOT and registration) and go up to around £4000 for a top-notch collectable model such as the Lambretta SX150. Accessories are attractively displayed and include chromed wheel covers and legshields, as well as helmets, badges, floor mats and a multitude of mirrors and lamps. A huge 'Vespa Servizio' sign hangs down from the ceiling, and the well-stocked two-ramp workshop at the back is more than able to handle all your after-sales needs.

Scooter Emporium

Address: 10 Dray Walk, The Old Truman Brewery, 91 Brick Lane, E1
Hours: Mon–Fri 08:30–18:00, Sat/Sun 10:30–16:00
Telephone: 020 7375 2277
Web: www.scooteremporium.com
Tube/rail: Aldgate East
Bus: 67

Over the years Marco has seen scooters go up and down in the fashion stakes, reaching a recent high in the mid-1990s when glossy mags such as *Vanity Fair* featured 'proud new owners' Robbie Williams and the Gallaghers. But the classic designs have never been out of favour with anyone who appreciates style, as well as the sheer practicality of getting around a city such as London on two wheels. A whole new generation of independent-minded commuters, notably from a media, fashion or arts background, now flock to the Emporium to test drive a new Vespa ET4 and linger over the vintage models.

Take your pick from the superb line-up of vintage Vespas and
Lambrettas at Scooter Emporium

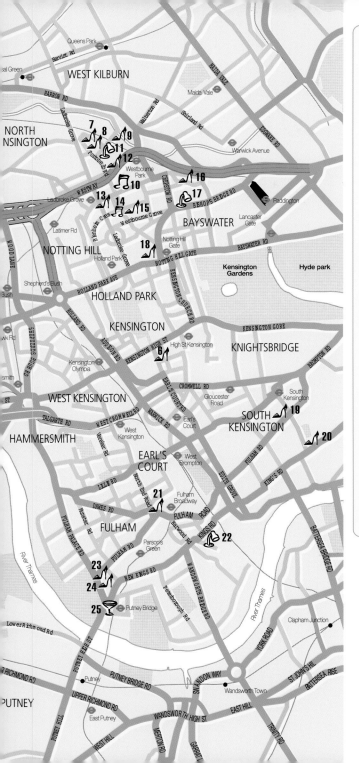

1. Reg Allen
2. Romance of Rust
3. Festival
4. Jukebox Showroom
5. The London Textile,
   Vintage Fashion and
   Accessories Fair
6. Orsini
7. '295'
8. The Antique Clothing Shop
9. Rellik
10. Intoxica
11. Flower Space
12. Portobello Road market
13. Still
14. Minus Zero & Stand Out
15. Sheila Cook
16. Appleby
17. The Reel Poster Gallery
18. Dolly Diamond
19. Butler & Wilson
20. Steinberg & Tolkien
21. TNT
22. De Parma
23. Circa
24. Old Hat
25. The River Café

● Railway Station
◉ Underground Station

west

167

For its classic interior and unfailing warm welcome this Fulham gem scores top marks. Locals have been coming for generations to enjoy the mix of traditional British food and added Latin character. Make mine a full English (or should that be a full Italian?).

FULHAM

Don't get this confused with that *other* River Café over in Thames Wharf. This one hasn't published a cookbook, doesn't look like an office, and, needless to say, is all the better for it. Here you'll find the welcoming sheen of formica table-tops and the lively clatter of patrons dispatching their 'daily specials'. With its vitrolite ceiling and blue-tiled walls, the dining room has changed little in the last 35 years. As with so many of London's surviving cafés and coffee shops from the 1950s and 1960s, this one has remained a family business – Italian, of course. Currently running the show are Liliana and her father, Lorenzo, who know the importance of good food, but also of preserving the River Café's special ambience. Customers come back time and again to chow down, chat, smoke, and read newspapers in surroundings that are all the more inviting for being so blissfully unmodernized.

The River Café

Address: 1 Station Approach, Fulham, SW6
Hours: Mon–Fri 07:00–17:00, Sat 07:00–15:00
Telephone: 020 7736 6296
Tube/rail: Putney Bridge
Bus: 14, 22, 220, 414, 430

A steady stream of 'Old Country' regulars adds a Latin flavour to the mix of diners, which varies widely at different times of the day. Thus, groups of clubbers stagger in craving hangover-cure fry-ups; tourists, bus drivers and local music-industry types keep the kitchen busy during lunch; and at weekends, families gather round to enjoy shepherd's pie and homemade apple crumble. A meal here with a cuppa on the side should come in at about four pounds; spend a whole fiver, and you'll need assistance getting to the door. As featured in pop videos and *The Bill*, this is a little bit of Fulham that – we hope – will be forever 1960s.

The original and still the best: Fulham's 'River Café' has been a home-from-home since the 60s

west: pad

From ceramics in Ealing, to jukeboxes in Acton, or film posters in Westbourne Park, West London enjoys more than its fair share of design one-of-a-kinds. Some of the most extraordinary items of all can be found lurking in a warehouse at the Fulham Gas Works.

ACTON

If, like me, you've always had a thing for a classic 1950s jukebox, then a visit to a shop like this – or even a glance at the window – should be followed by a cold shower. RockOlas, Seebergs, NSMs and AMIs are all lined up and looking every bit as good as on the day they left the factory. The designs embody the excitement, imagination and sheer flair of the rock'n'roll era, with chrome trimmings modelled on car bumpers, display panels curved like windscreens, and domes with flashing lights inspired by passing UFOs.

Brothers Steve and Ray have between them no less than half a century of experience buying, selling and reviving these marvellous machines. Their showroom in Acton boasts a mixture of vintage models and modern, but classically styled designs. Many of the older examples have already found a buyer by the time they appear in the showroom – and no wonder: to get this far they've already undergone a minimum of 500 hours painstaking restoration work. Each machine is stripped down to its smallest components – nuts, bolts, tiny slivers of Plexiglas and chrome – before being rebuilt from scratch. Steve and Ray's workshop is a treasure trove of spare parts amassed over the years, the likes of which would be impossible to replicate; but even so, many items have to be re-made by hand.

At a cost of anything from five to ten thousand pounds these beauties don't

Jukebox Showroom

Address: 9 Park Parade, Gunnersbury Avenue, Acton, W3
Hours: Mon–Tues & Thurs–Sat 10:30-18:00; Wed & Sun by appointment
Telephone: 020 8992 8482
Web: www.jukeboxshowroom.co.uk
Tube/rail: Acton Town
Bus: E3

Heaven at 45rpm! This beautiful RockOla is what pop was made for, and is increasingly prized today

come cheap. But the going rates are actually very fair, given the sheer scale of the labour involved. On top of which there is the brothers' unique expertise and artistry, which it would be difficult to price. They can even help supply some suitable sounds, with a stock of no less than 25,000 seven-inch singles for buyers to choose from. As Steve and Ray put it so succinctly: 'Don't dream it: own it!'

EALING

T he US may have patented rock'n'roll, but when it comes to ceramics, Britain led the world in the 1950s. To find out more about that legacy – and even buy a bit of it to take home – there are few better places to visit than South Ealing's Festival. The name itself is a canny evocation of that great high point of post-war regeneration, the 1951 Festival of Britain. Nowhere was the new decade's growing sense of optimism more apparent than in the field of art and design, and within a few years of the Skylon's appearance on the South Bank, Britain's potteries were turning out a steady stream of bold, imaginative and affordable new lines.

Festival

Address: 136 South Ealing Rd, W5
Hours: Mon–Sat 10:00–17:30
Telephone: 020 8840 9333
Web: www.festival1951.demon.co.uk
Tube/rail: South Ealing
Bus: 65, E3

Portmeirion coffee pots

Owner Steve Jenkins has written widely on ceramics, and has built up an enviable reputation. A particular passion is Midwinter, and it's not hard to see why. House designer Jessie Tait created a whole string of highly successful patterns, from the stripes of Zambezi to the stylized leaves of Primavera. The same company also produced some of Terence Conran's earliest designs –

the 'Nature Study' series from 1955 – along with the delightful 'Riviera' collection by Hugh Casson. Sir Hugh's stylish drawings of pavement cafés and sea-front flower-sellers brought a little burst of Mediterranean life into homes up and down the land, and were perfectly in tune with the aspirations of the time.

Talking to Steve is an instant education, and his enthusiasm for his subject is infectious. Collectors the world over now come to him in search of plates, coffee cups, jugs, cruet sets, bowls and ladles dating from the 1930s to the 1970s. Of the earlier designs, those by Susie Cooper are especially sought after, whilst there is always demand for Portmeirion, Denby Arabesque, Poole, and Beswick's magical 'Circus'. Not only the decorations, but the forms themselves are often very distinctive, such as the so-called 'fashion' and 'style-craft' shapes, combining square bottoms and rounded tops to great effect. Some of the best known patterns of all are also the most affordable, notably Enid Seeney's 'Homemaker' with its black-and-white graphics of 1950s furniture. Not everything at Festival is British, as there are classics from Scandinavia too, and prices range from under a tenner to several hundred pounds. But be warned: this stuff is addictive.

FULHAM

De Parma is out of the ordinary in every sense. First, there's the location. 'The Gas Works' address is not some swanky redeveloped site, but a still very busy industrial facility, complete with men in boiler suits and swarms of Transco vans. Some of the buildings have been rented out to small businesses and dealers, who now make this perhaps the most 'alternative' retail park in London. De Parma itself occupies part of a warehouse at the far end of the works,

De Parma

Address: Core 1, The Gas Works, 2 Michael Rd, SW6
Hours: 'Not early till late'
Telephone: 07976 280275
Web: www.deparma.com
Tube/rail: Fulham Broadway
Bus: 11, 22, 391, C3

and extra fun can be had on the way back by finding someone has locked you in (as I discovered). On the plus side, the gasometers themselves look great in close-up (design classics if ever I saw them).

Just as extraordinary as the setting is De Parma's eclectic and highly unusual stock. Many of the items here are not to be found anywhere else in town (or if they are, then they're well hidden!). A good example is Jorgen Hovelskov's remarkable

'Harp' chair from 1968, which not only resembles its namesake, but also incorporates witty references to its Danish origins: its profile echoes the high, curving bow of a longboat, whilst the taut strings that form the seat turn out to be nautical flag-line. And yes, it *is* comfortable to sit on.

50s design meets Dr. Caligari!

Items are mostly from the 1930s to the 1970s, with the pre-war period as readily represented by early modernist designs as by luscious late deco. There are design legends a-plenty – George Nelson, Alvar Aalto – but also much with that 'wow' factor without the help of a famous name. An unattributed 1950s dressing table in orange and black, with wild, almost expressionist angles and trapezoid drawers, is a match for many a better catalogued number. Owner Gary de Sparham sums it all up as 'quality, interesting, antique stuff', and his own current favourite happens to be a 1930s French table with chromed sides and black mirror-glass top. A design book of the time described it as fit 'to please the most fastidious mind', and I'm not one to disagree.

Apart from the furniture, the lighting also throws up some surprises. For sheer fun, top prize goes to Prof Angelo Brutto's 1970 Drumlight (£1,750) that displays a jumble of multicoloured abstract shapes through its semi-transparent skin. Turn the wall-mounted frame, and you can roll the shapes into a new arrangement, rather like a psychedelic light-show in slow motion. Of course, all this flair and innovation doesn't come cheap, and some of the items here sell for more than £20,000. But where comparisons can be made, the prices are actually very fair. What is most refreshing is that such a high-end stock is presented in a relaxed and light-hearted way. As far as Gary is concerned, 'life is too important to be taken seriously'; and above all, De Parma embodies a spirit of fun and adventure, which is perhaps the best possible tribute to the designers whose work we now so admire.

LADBROKE GROVE

Flower Space brings a welcome dash of post-war design to an area that is better known for its traditional antiques. Up at the north end of Portobello Road, Flower Space nestles among stores that sell everything from vintage vinyl to homemade falafels (a perfect, if unusual, combination!). Since starting up a couple of years ago, Dale, Sandra and Les have built up a strong local following who appreciate the shop's eclectic mix and relaxed, good-natured ambience.

Flower Space

Address: 301 Portobello Rd, W10
Hours: Mon 11:00–18:00, Tues–Thurs by appointment, Fri-Sat 10:00–18:00, Sun 12:00–16:00
Telephone: 020 8968 9966
Tube/rail: Ladbroke Grove
Bus: 7, 23, 52, 70

Prices range from £3 to £3000, or in other words from a tomato-shaped ketchup bottle to a Perspex hanging chair on a chrome, egg-shaped frame. (Just add some Francis Bacon for the complete decorative-arts fry-up!) The range of lighting is extensive, and Flower Space is particularly good for Castiglioni's Arco lamps – the ones with great sweeping arms that curve up from a heavy base and extend about 10 feet across the room. These are all European originals, mostly from the 1970s, and sell for between three and eight hundred pounds. Regulars also expect to find some unusual film posters on the walls, such as Blaxploitation classic *Cotton Comes to Harlem* or a 'chase' for *2001* (that's a kind of small warm-up ad that came out before the official campaign, and consequently is pretty rare today).

Lights fantastic at 'Flower Space'

Stock selection is more about the overall look than particular designers' names, and it can only be a good sign that Italian *Vogue* are always borrowing things for shoots; soul diva Des'ree even shot a video in the store. If you're not sure whether something will look right when you get it home, then simply ask to try it out first. Dale and Sandra would rather have a satisfied customer than a quick one-off sale.

NOTTING HILL

F rom the moment they met it was murder!' So announced the original US poster for *Double Indemnity*, one of the all-time cinema greats. But films have always been promoted very differently around the world, and in this case punters in Spain were lured by an image of Billy Wilder's original ending, with Fred MacMurray sent to the

The Reel Poster Gallery

Address: 72 Westbourne Grove, W2
Hours: Mon–Fri 11:00–19:00, Sat 12:00–18:00
Telephone: 020 7727 4488
Web: www.reelposter.com
Tube/rail: Royal Oak/Notting Hill Gate
Bus: 7, 23, 27, 70

electric chair. Such variations can be fun to ferret out, but would perhaps be of little lasting interest were it not for the fact that the posters themselves are so stunning. At their best they are an art form in their own right, and if you need any convincing, then a trip to Westbourne Grove should do the trick.

The gallery itself is a bright and spacious room with about a dozen posters on display at any one time. Filling one wall might be an image from Antonioni, boasting a radiant Monica Vitti *life-sized*, and next to it a floor-to-ceiling scene from some pre-war melodrama showing Gary Cooper glowering at a weak-kneed starlet. On a smaller scale, there's James Dean billed in Japanese, Christopher Lee baring his fangs, and Robbie the Robot looking none too pleased at being next to Bergman's Persona. In the centre of all this drama is a group of chairs and a coffee table piled high with ring binders, and you can open any one of these to get a glimpse of the wider stock – at the last count this amounted to more than 12,000 posters. This treasure trove includes just about every movie you've ever heard of, and a whole lot more besides. Certain countries or certain periods really stand out. Take Eastern Europe, where the tradition for radical imagery has long been a source of delight (the NFT once used to have an all-Polish display outside its main entrance). Or there's film noir, a house speciality, which gave rise to some of the most eye-catching and visually sensational artwork of all.

Founders Bruce Marchant and Tony Nourmand are internationally renowned authorities on their subject, with a clutch of books to their names. Their emphasis when selecting stock is very much on design, and all the items are original, not reproductions. Prices start at less than a ton for recent Disney releases or Brit-hits such as *Trainspotting*, whilst a real classic such as Burt Lancaster's *The Swimmer* can be had for a mere £350. In a highly collectable market the true stunners will tend to set you back a few grand, and for sheer desirability few can compete with Dziga Vertov's *Man With a Movie Camera*. The poster is as much a piece of history as the film itself, and when one last reached the market it sold for a seismic £50,000.

West London rides high in the vintage fashion stakes, with Notting Hill alone boasting a whole trousseau of world class stores. Equally unmissable are the famous names and gilt-edged selections of nearby Chelsea.

CHELSEA

Fans of costume jewellery need no introduction to Butler & Wilson, who are world renowned for their sometimes bold, always beautiful designs. In recent years the company has become equally well known for its range of vintage items, from trademark sparklies and accessories to a suitably glamorous line-up of clothing. These can all be found at the Fulham Road store, where the window displays of pristine flapper dresses and jewel-bedecked busts have long been a source of wonderment to passers-by.

Butler & Wilson

Address: 189 Fulham Rd, SW3
Hours: Mon–Sat 10:00-18:00 (Wed till 19:00), Sun 12:00–18:00
Telephone: 020 7352 3045
Web: www.butlerandwilson.co.uk
Tube/rail: South Kensington
Bus: 14, 49, 211, 345, 414

Chandeliers, pier glasses and gilt balustrades add to the sense of opulence – and yet the shop remains entirely welcoming, with knowledgeable and attentive staff. Taking centre stage are great cabinets of jewellery, mostly vintage but with some sympathetic contemporary designs. Name hunters are treated to superb examples by Haggler, Haskell and Trifari, whilst the overall selection is varied enough to satisfy all tastes. As well as the trays of brooches in enamel, diamanté and glass, there are earrings of every size and shape, bracelets, chokers, and a whole raft of necklaces that spill out across the counter and on to the mannequins nearby. Prices start at under £20 and rise to several hundred, though something special can usually be secured for under three figures.

The first floor is reached by way of a spectacular display of vintage bags, pinned to the wall in their hundreds along the entire length of the staircase. At the top is

Mexican circle skirts can be twinned with top-notch vintage bags
and costume jewellery at Butler & Wilson

a boudoir-ish room filled with jackets, shirts, coats and more, dating from the 1920s to the 1970s. All are in excellent condition, and the popular beaded dresses are nothing short of museum quality, though most are bought to wear, rather than to file away. The sleek 1930s gowns look at once period perfect and utterly cutting edge, whilst the 1950s circle skirts are perennial favourites, especially the Mexican hand-made variety. A standout feature is the selection of traditional and richly embroidered Far Eastern silk jackets, many of which once served a ceremonial purpose, but now make the perfect attire for a sophisticated night out. Customers love the eclectic range of styles, and enjoy putting together their own individual look, whether for daywear, the evening or something in-between.

Perhaps the most unusual items in the shop are the 1950s wicker handbags in wild designs of fish, elephant heads, or even little monkeys complete with lipstick and skirt! These are extremely rare and consequently aren't cheap, but for sheer entertainment value they are not to be missed.

Steinberg & Tolkien has been a feature on the King's Road for over 10 years. The sheer quantity of stock is remarkable, as is its variety. Womenswear of almost every type can be found here, and from all eras, the only downside being that very little room is left for the guys (who make do with braces, ties and cufflinks).

Steinberg & Tolkien

Address: 193 King's Rd, SW3
Hours: Mon–Sat 11:00–19:00, Sun 12:00–18:00
Telephone: 020 7376 3660
Tube/rail: South Kensington/Sloane Square
Bus: 11, 19, 22, 49, 319

The layout of the shop brings together most clothing essentials in a suite of rooms downstairs, whilst the ground floor has pretty much everything else, including accessories and cabinets of luscious costume jewellery. Hanging on the walls are enough dresses, coats, skirts and jackets to give a taste of what lies below. Many are adorned with large hand-written signs that read like a *Who's Who* of twentieth-century fashion: Courrèges, Schiaparelli, Chanel, Dior, Pucci and a host of British designers from Bill Blass and Vivienne Westwood to Ossie Clarke and 'Mr. Freedom'. Here, too, are showcased occasional curiosities, such as the 1960s psychedelic dress by 'James Sterling *Paper* Fashions', complete with instruction leaflet telling us it's 'flame proof and washable'.

Downstairs are rail upon rail of tightly packed ball gowns, summer frocks and cocktail dresses, double-stacked skirts, blouses and anything else a fashionable wardrobe might require. The colours are exquisite, with spotlights further brightening a lemon yellow here or a rose pink there at the back. Meanwhile, dozens of little black numbers grouped in one corner make a perfect exercise in variations on a theme. Anything that overstays its welcome eventually heads into the large separate 'sale room' at the back (which is always worth a browse).

The staff could not be more friendly, and obviously love the things they sell. Their assistance can be invaluable in locating just the right thing, or teaming up the perfect match. Customers range from passing teens to museums, film companies, models, tourists, and just about anyone else who appreciates beautifully made clothes. Brides are increasingly keen to tie the knot in something a little different, whether it's a 1930s full-length gown or a cute, full-skirted 1950s number. And trendspotters take note:

Unmissable Steinberg

even hats are on the up, especially the daintier, easy-to-wear variety with little veils. All in all, S&T is a must-see – just don't expect to see *everything* in one trip!

FULHAM

F or fans of beautiful vintage womenswear, Circa is a treat. Every item in the shop is there for a very good reason: it might be the cut, the fabric, or some amazing appliqué design, just as long as the lucky wearer will look her glamorous best. As for dates, owner Marianne and her daughter Astral are happy to cast their net far and wide, from Victoriana to the relatively recent

Circa

Address: 8 Fulham High St, SW6
Hours: Mon–Fri 11.00–18.00, Sat 11.00–17.00
Telephone: 020 7736 5038
Tube/Rail: Putney Bridge
Bus: 14, 22, 220, 414, 430

Clothes to cherish at Circa

past. The result is a vibrant and eclectic mix of pre-war chiffons and Edwardian beaded gowns, along with ever-fashionable cocktail dresses, gossamer summer numbers and elegant eveningwear from the 1950s and 1960s.

Great care is taken with display. Padded hangers and uncrammed rails help to individualize the clothes, as does the clever use of mannequins and wall space, whilst the red plush sofa positively invites a quiet moment of reflection. Standouts include a selection of Mexican circle skirts, with exquisite designs of palm-fringed beaches and couples serenaded by mariachis (£150–£350). Other eye-catchers include ruffled bolero jackets, peignoirs, a lovely Martini-label print, and an Art Nouveau dress, liberally fringed and beaded, with asymmetrical hem and fabulous coiled-snake motif. Label hunters will not be disappointed, with the likes of Dior and Givenchy putting in a regular appearance along with major British names such as Zandra Rhodes and Jeff Banks. Prices reflect the condition and quality of the clothes on offer, but always with a view to what's fair and affordable. Blouses start from around £60 and dresses more like £80, with many deservedly fetching three figures.

The single room has a raised area towards the back, which harbours a fine stash of accessories ranging from mules and kitten heels, to cloche hats, fedoras, bags, gloves, shawls and even occasional 1950s swimsuits (which have been featured in *Vogue*). The shop as a whole is one big showcase, but for no more than perhaps a tenth of the total stock at Marianne's command – which means that for specific requests there is every chance of just the thing being summoned up from some hidden recess.

Chock full of such one-time essentials as plus-fours, toppers, riding boots and caps, Old Hat is a homage to an age when men wore tweed and women baked cakes. The shop has become an institution with local 'Fulham men', for whom everyday wear has changed little since the 1950s. But the stock appeals equally to those dapper types whose idea of vintage style tends more towards the pre-war Prince of Wales than Steve McQueen or Elvis.

Old Hat

Address: 66 & 43A Fulham High St, SW6
Hours: Daily 11:00-19:00
Telephone: 020 7610 6558
Tube/rail: Putney Bridge
Bus: 14, 22, 220, 414, 430

Items date from the 1950s to the present, though the timeless cuts could easily be much older. There's a nice line in hefty overcoats, blazers and formal wear, as well as some natty 1970s velvet suits in striped, bottle-green fabric (£75)

As well as the two jam-packed rooms of menswear, there are treasures for the

An age of tweeds and toppers is evoked at Old Hat

girls, notably suits and dresses by Chanel, original Courrèges, and assorted couture classics. But these are kept separately a few doors along, and are best viewed by appointment.

Owner David Saxby runs two similar stores in Tokyo, but somehow he also finds time to write a regular column for quirky mag *The Chap*, where the sartorially perplexed seek his advice on everything from collar studs to spats. Look out, too, for David's marquee at the hugely successful Goodwood revival meetings, where dressing up is a big part of the fun.

T NT claims to have sold Kylie her famous hot pants, but the lady herself, sorry to say, can't seem to remember. One thing's for sure, if it's hot pants you want, then this is the place to come. The fun element is to the fore here and the shop is – to quote the flyers – 'a colourful haven of 60s, 70s, 80s, flower power, glam rock and disco clothing'. Budding Abigails are bowled over by the 1970s wide-legged trouser suits and billowing gowns, whilst 1960s items likewise extend to the full-on 'Austin Powers' end of the spectrum, which many a more 'serious' store might avoid.

But in among the sequins and the lamé are occasional real gems that could hold their own in any company. Show-stoppers on my last visit were a pair of dresses fully deserving of their window showcase. Expertly tailored in 1960s Hong Kong, their elegant, full-length silhouettes perfectly offset the vibrant period fabrics. And at £85 each they would surely have been snatched up long since if they hadn't been a small size 8. Just under half the stock is menswear, from flares and velvet jackets to sensible shoes and suits.

TNT

Address: 14 Jerdan Place, SW6
Hours: Mon–Sat 11:00–18:00, Sun 12:00–16:00
Telephone: 020 7385 2062
Tube/rail: Fulham Broadway
Bus: 14, 28, 211, 295, 414

TNT's 60s showstoppers

The shop reflects the character of its owner Tass (pronounced 'Taz'), who takes his name from the tassels that once decorated his drum kit. A boardful of badges by the door draws on his huge personal collection and amounts to a pictorial history of 1960s and 1970s pop. (Rod Stewart fans take note!) In business for over 30 years and here since the mid-1990s, Tass appreciates classic clothes, but also likes to help people have a good time. TNT has long been a port of call for regulars at 1970s-night 'Carwash', and is perfectly placed to deal with a whole new generation of Starskies, Hutches, and even Huggy Bears.

HAMMERSMITH

The London Textile, Vintage Fashion and Accessories Fair is the premier event of its kind, and underlines the role of London as a major fashion hub. For this, fair organizer Paola deserves our applause, bringing together as she does upwards of 100 leading dealers several times a year.

The building is packed tight with wearables of every imaginable kind. There are hats, handbags and jewellery side by side with lace, beadwork, couture and embroidery, all dating from around 1800 to 1980. Bargains, rarities, and even downright oddities all exert their appeal, and prices range from just a few pounds to hundreds. With so many vintage-lovers under one roof there is a real buzz of excitement, and at every turn one hears approving gasps or encounters people hurriedly trying on a shawl or fabulous gown.

The dealers range from all-encompassing generalists to finely tuned specialists, whether by era or by type. Charlotte Taylor, for example, sells fabrics from the 1920s to the 1970s, all beautifully displayed in neat little rolls. Most of the time she deals direct with designers and film companies, but at this, her only public outlet, she gives

The London Textile, Vintage Fashion & Accessories Fair

Address: Hammersmith Town Hall, King St, W6
Hours: Occasional Sundays approximately every six weeks, 10:00–17:00
Telephone: 020 8543 5075 (organizer, Paola)
Web: www.pa-antiques.co.uk
Tube/rail: Ravenscourt Park
Bus: 27, 190, 267, 391, H91

A blue-riband event

the rest of us a chance to get our hands on yards of pristine materials, and perhaps kit out a little 1930s costume drama of our own. Others have made a lengthy trip from as far away as Liverpool, Harrogate or, in the case of Maggie Lee, from Exmouth, bringing with her a whole shop's worth of costume jewellery (and some jazzy one-piece swimsuits for good measure). Travelling up from points west are two Alexandras, Cunha and Fairweather, respectively offering delightful blouson-style Victorian jackets, and a fine selection of vintage evening dresses. Meanwhile, local Daisy Jellicoe always wins fans with her stock of bargain 1950s dresses. She likes to have them all piled up and looking like jumble, until the quickest rummage reveals fashionable flared skirts and summer prints, for between £15 and £25. Other Londoners with shops nearby often save their best pieces for fairs such as this, as in the case of 'What the Butler Wore', proudly showing off their Biba.

Early birds can enjoy the relative calm before the p.m. rush and the pick of the crop. Paola has strict criteria for inclusion, and the quality of the show is never less than tip-top. Celeb-spotters will have a field day, too – though really, no amount of famous faces can compete with the clothes. Just wandering the aisles is an education, and only the strongest of wills (or the strangest of tastes) will fail to take home a treat.

KENSINGTON

O rsini has long been a feature at the north end of Earl's Court Road. The shop has recently undergone a transformation, and new owner Sophie has introduced a lighter, fresher feel, with more emphasis on wearability and glamour. Flowers, screens and lacquered cabinets lend the main room a gentle opulence, whilst the clothes themselves are attractively displayed on padded

Orsini

Address: 76 Earl's Court Rd, W8
Hours: Mon 12:00–18:00, Tues-Sat 11:00–19:00
Telephone: 020 7937 2903
Tube/rail: High St, Kensington
Bus: 328, C1

hangers and with sufficient space for each to make its case. The result is a shop that appeals more to fashion-conscious buyers than those of a theatrical persuasion (though film and TV companies are always welcome!).

A little of the old stock remains, and Sophie intends to reserve a place on the rails for outstanding pieces of Victoriana and turn-of-the-century capes in gorgeous fabrics (£70–£100, with more to choose from in winter). But in keeping with the glamour theme, the 1930s and 1950s now make the strongest showing. Among the pre-war pieces, current prize-winners include Chinese silk pyjama suits, and a fabulous 1930s evening dress in shimmering bronze satin complete with matching cape and diamante clasp, fully deserving its £300 price tag. Alongside are lovely chiffon day dresses, and a selection of hats (£45–£60).

Beaded bags are another house speciality, with dozens to choose from (£35–£85), whilst underwear also gets more than its usual share of the limelight. Silk sets from the 1940s are especially popular, and there are plans to introduce a range of reproduction flimsies in the near future. From the 1950s there's a tremendous all-round line-up, from sleeveless summer dresses in pretty prints (£50) to lavish evening gowns in lipstick pinks, and ice-cream greens with yards of rustling net. Don't miss the 1950s women's shirts, too, as Sophie has conjured up some fantastic dead-stock items with period details such as capped sleeves, little raised collars and tailored waists, all in classic fabrics that say 'Take me to Capri, Daddy-o, and don't forget your sax!'.

LADBROKE GROVE

From its polished wooden floor to its parachute-draped ceiling, this is a shop with character. In the bright first room I particularly liked the ladies' heads from pre-war hairdressers, now happily sporting a variety of felt hats and sunglasses. Alongside them is a large collection of menswear, including shirts – plain, striped or Hawaiian – suits, cuff-links, hats for under £10, and indestructible Harris Tweed jackets for around £15. The look is casual, man-about-town circa 1960, and appeals as much to the Japanese student stocking up on loungewear as to the elderly gent bemoaning the demise of Dunn & Co. Prices for womenswear are just as

295

Address: 295 Portobello Rd, W10
Hours: Fri/Sat 8:30–17:00
Telephone: No telephone
Tube/rail: Ladbroke Grove
Bus: 7, 23, 52, 70

295 has character to spare

reasonable, with 1960s dresses starting at less than £10 for a simple cotton shift, and rising to the giddy heights of £20 for a more elaborate evening number.

Stock is mostly '1970s backwards', though the older items tend not to hang around for too long. More than anything else, the sheer variety on offer at 295 is what gives it a special charm. Vintage swimwear, for example, is not exactly easy to find, but here you can take your pick from a whole lidoful of one-piece Esther Williams' numbers in natty checks or bold 1970s designs. Some of them would make fantastic club gear! There are also silk dressing gowns and slips, blouses and braces, and even some neat little outfits for retro kids. Go through to the back of the shop and there's a small room where you will find costume jewellery and an unusually large and very popular selection of vintage lingerie.

Customers range from teens to silver surfers, and include all the usual fashion scouts, designers and canny socialites who know a good thing when they see it.

Opened in 1993, this is one of those shops that feels like it's been around for ever. Owner Sandy Stagg likes to create the impression of a 'junk shop', but it is one where everything on inspection turns out to be top notch.

Sandy has been in the business for more than 30 years, and sums up her wares as 'pre-1970s costume and accessories'. In practice this means a focus on very wearable styles from the 1920s to the 1950s, with occasional

The Antique Clothing Shop

Address: 282 Portobello Rd, W10
Hours: Fri/Sat 9:00–18:00
Telephone: 020 8964 4830
Tube/rail: Ladbroke Grove
Bus: 7, 23, 52, 70

1960s items, and even some Victoriana. For the women there are feminine chiffon tea-dresses from £150, and a huge range of 1950s numbers, from cotton daywear in colourful prints to gorgeous evening gowns (all from £30–£80). Accessories include shoes, gloves and umbrellas from just about every era, but also a vast horde of feathers, hat veils, buttons, braids and trims.

Guys are not forgotten either, with part of the shop devoted to dark wood shelves and glass-fronted drawers straight out of a pre-war gentleman's outfitters. Striped blazers, collarless shirts, demob suits, braces, cravats and military regalia are all hugely popular, and Sandy would stock more if she could find them!

Catwalk trends come and go with dizzying speed, but whatever the latest look, Sandy prides herself on having the originals – from peasant blouses, leg-of-mutton sleeves or Suzie Wong dresses, to a seemingly endless supply of beautiful 1950s sweaters. She's also the owner of The Vintage Home Store in Acton; she spends the early part of the week there, and offers a good line in vintage fabrics (including some classic 1950s designs for the perfect retro cushions and curtains).

The shop in Portobello opens only on Fridays and Saturdays, which means it can get very busy, especially in the summer months. Arrive early to be sure of a really good look round.

J ust North of the Westway, Portobello Market boasts some excellent vintage clothing dealers every bit as likely as their indoor neighbours to be offering real gems. Do bear in mind that some of them are present for only one day of the market, and exact locations can vary.

Stallholders to the west find shelter under a permanent canopy, whilst those to the east make do with more traditional weatherproofing.

Portobello Road Market

Address: Portobello Rd, junction with Cambridge Gardens & Acklam Rd, W10
Hours: Fri & Sat 08:00-17:00
Tube/rail: Ladbroke Grove
Bus: 7, 23, 52, 70

First port of call is **Vivien**, who occupies a spot on the corner of Acklam Road and stocks a selection of well chosen womenswear. Dates, styles and fabrics are all equally wide ranging, and when I last saw her, at the Battersea Vintage Fashion Fair, her showstoppers were a couple of amazing nineteenth-century corsets in rich embroidered silks, complete with royal warrant inside.

Almost opposite are two of the area's most colourful characters, Caspar and Peter, who together run the thriving micro-business called **A Dandy in Aspic**. This is a mecca for Mods and 1960s stylists, including many of the hardcore perfectionists who only buy the best. Caspar recalls the guy who came to try on boots,

Flower power at A Dandy in Aspic

and when offered the use of a shoe-horn promptly reached into a pocket and pulled out his own. A dandy indeed! But anyone with a taste for classic vintage fashion will enjoy the range of sharp suits, velvet and satin mini-dresses, hipsters and period-perfect chisel-toed shoes. Highly collectable 1960s labels can also usually be had, including Mary Quant, Biba, Bus Stop, Mr Fish and the legendary Granny Takes A Trip. This is especially true on Saturdays when the stall is joined by Angie and her **Too Much Boutique**. Caspar meanwhile can often be found in his evening DJ guise at suitably smart venues such as The Pleasure Unit.

Cross the road to Cambridge Gardens, for the stalls of **Jimmy** and Anton. The first stands out for his imaginative range of womenswear, much of it on the older side of average. Delightful 1940s dresses come in classic prints or sheer two-tone cotton, and include several war-time numbers complete with 'CC41' labels, all priced at around £50. Given the constraints of the time, these 'Civilian Clothing' designs consistently surprise with their clever, economic details and flattering, well tailored cuts. Another of Jimmy's specialities are 1930s bed jackets, which prove very popular as evening wear or twinned with jeans for a stylish individual look.

A few yards away is fellow regular, **Anton**, who divides his space equally between men's and women's garments. For the guys there are shirts, coats, suits and some pre-war dinner wear (with incredibly weighty cloth). Ladies meanwhile get to choose from a top-notch selection of dresses, including some real standouts from the 1940s and 1950s, with fashionable polka dots, halter necks, geometric prints and a host of period details such as bows and capped sleeves; there's many a shi shi shop that would be proud to offer items as good as this. Anton also stocks things from the 1960s and occasionally the 1970s, but draws the line at the 1980s on grounds of taste. The 1950s numbers typically sell for as little as £25/£30, and the only things to break into three figures are the superb minks, including coats and short capes. Just the thing for a typical English summer!

Rellik is not so much a shop as a phenomenon, name-checked in countless celebrity interviews, and courted by the style pundits of the world. Rarely does a retail space exude such a palpable sense of 'being where it's at'. The atmosphere is further charged by the personalities of owners Steven, Fiona and Claire, who each make their own distinctive contribution to Rellik's three-pronged attack.

Rellik

Address: 8 Golborne Rd, W10
Hours: Tues–Sat 10:00–18:00
Telephone: 020 8962 0089
Tube/rail: Westbourne Park
Bus: 23

Steven mis-spent his early 1980s youth in the company of Leigh Bowery, Andrew Logan and the other satraps of London's post-punk club scene. He now offers a huge range of original items from those heady days, along with pieces by earlier British designers such as Bill Gibb, Thea Porter, Zandra Rhodes and Ossie Clarke. Most sought-after of all are the Vivienne Westwoods, which command a fanatical and deep-pocketed global following. All the seminal designs are here, from those notorious platform shoes to the legendary 'Seditionaries' T-shirts complete with safety pins or cruising cowboys. Collectors and pop stars have been known to pay £1000 or more for something really special, but fortunately for the rest of us there are reproductions too – quite good enough for looking the part at ultra-hip, 1980s revivalist hangouts such as Nag, Nag, Nag.

Claire, on the other hand, is the 'customize queen', with a knack for 'modernizing' vintage items and making them her own. She's equally happy to leave them as they are, just as long as they have real character and are eminently wearable. As far as she's concerned 'a successful sale is something that's worn a lot' – and her loyal customers seem to have no trouble doing just that.

Fiona likewise is keen to bring out the modern-day potential of vintage items by way of some imaginative updating, turning a 1930s housecoat, for example, into a stunning blouse. Her starting point

Razor-sharp Rellik

could be any era, but the end result is guaranteed to be an exercise in up-to-the-minute fashion. The shop itself makes something of a statement by being down at the 'wrong end' of Portobello – not that this deters the steady stream of style fans who rank this as one of the capital's most essential destinations.

Prices offer little cause for alarm, unless one insists on collectable labels. A complete outfit can be had for a budget of £100, which is less than dinner for two at many a nearby nose-bag

Still's large windows are remarkably uncluttered, with usually just one or two dresses displayed dead-centre on simple tailor's dummies. This allows you to see right into the shop's interior, which is bright and enticing. But it also means you really get to notice all the details of the showcased items — the cut, the fabric, that little kick-pleat or buttoned cuff, and even the delicate embroidery that could so easily have been missed.

By the time you step inside you'll be perfectly attuned to Still's way of doing things, which is to value every item of clothing for its own distinctive merits. This makes for a delightfully eclectic mix. Examples of superbly crafted knitwear or antique leather sit alongside 1950s summer dresses in gorgeous floral organza (from £100), which, like everything else in the shop, are in tip-top condition with utterly reliable zips! Here, too, are wearable gems from as far back as the mid-nineteenth-century, such as a cotton petticoat or pair of riding boots, whilst more recent standouts include classic 1980s suits by Thierry Mugler (£175), and even a few contemporary pieces by designers using vintage materials. The bulk of the stock

Still

Address: 61d Lancaster Rd, W11
Hours: Mon–Fri 11:00–18:00, Sat 10:30–18:30, Sun 12:00–16:00
Telephone: 020 7243 2932
Tube/rail: Ladbroke Grove
Bus: 7, 70

Attention to detail at 'Still'

at any one time is actually hidden out of sight, the better to appreciate what's hanging on the rails. Decoration is also subtle and unobtrusive, with small film-noir posters adding just enough of a period touch.

Owner Sophie has been collecting vintage clothing since she was 13, and clearly loves the things she sells. She particularly enjoys the variety and quality of the fabrics, as well as the huge colour range offered by past decades. Among her recent favourites was an exquisite 1920s dress in lilac linen with hand-embroidered deco motifs (£185). Just as memorable were the 1970s dresses made by Yuki from a single piece of jersey (very Grecian, and very flattering). Label hunters might find something by Jean Muir or Jeff Banks, but the emphasis here is very much on the look, rather than the provenance. For anyone who appreciates beautifully made and expertly selected clothing, Still is quite simply a must.

NOTTING HILL

W hen it comes to vintage clothing, Notting Hill has an embarrassment of riches, and this is one shop that absolutely should not be missed; the window displays alone are worth the trip. On my last visit there was a traffic-stopping trio of stunning 1950s gowns in calf-length silks and chiffons, beautifully posed and accessorized, and set against a backdrop of life-sized period fashion drawings that mirrored their elegant shapes. The whole arrangement could have come straight from the pages of *Vogue*, *circa* 1957.

Dolly Diamond

Address: 51 Pembridge Rd, Notting Hill Gate, W11
Hours: Mon-Sat 10:30-18:30, Sun 12:00–18:00
Telephone: 020 7792 2479
Web: www.dollydiamond.com
Tube/rail: Notting Hill Gate
Bus: 27, 28, 31, 328

The clothes inside are every bit as exciting. With twenty years' experience to call upon, Dolly knows exactly what her customers want. Most recently, the revival of full skirts and grown-up party wear, coupled with the influence of 'Sex & The City', has stoked up interest in 1950s originals that were, in any case, always in demand. Prices average £75–£125 for dresses that range from sleeveless brocade numbers to floral organza, floaty chocolate-coloured confections, and diagonal-striped pink and black gowns complete with *I Love Lucy* collars.

But the stock as a whole appeals to more than just the budding Audrey

Hepburns and Grace Kellys. Sleek 1930s gowns in georgette are fast becoming favourites with bridesmaids or even the occasional bride, whilst Victorian blouses and 1920s beaded dresses share rails with romantic 1970s classics, and even occasional standouts from the 1980s. Whatever the era, the emphasis is on glamour, though not at the cost of wearability. Prices, too, are very fair for items that are in superb condition and among the very best of their kind.

In a second room upstairs there is a good selection of menswear including shirts and ties, hats, evening wear, frockcoats and classic striped blazers (that never stay around for long). Accessories for both men and women are a real strength, and are a further draw for the designers and enthusiasts who come from far and wide. There are also hidden storage rooms where more treasures are tucked carefully away, and gladly retrieved for the asking. A delight from start to finish…

Sheila Cook ranks as one of the doyennes of the vintage clothing world: her knowledge is encyclopaedic, and her stock equally wide ranging. Sheila takes whole centuries on board, quite happily showcasing a dress from the 1740s alongside a Dior knitted jacket or an early nineteenth-century military uniform.

Unifying themes are beauty, condition, character and quality of

Sheila Cook

Address: 184 Westbourne Grove, W11
Hours: By appointment
Telephone: 020 7792 8001
Web: www.sheilacook.co.uk
Tube/rail: Notting Hill Gate
Bus: 23

design, and these are traced through countless varieties of costume up to the 1970s. Along the way customers can expect to find gems such as a 1920s lamé shawl, Biba seersucker trousers, or pieces by Thea Porter and Ossie Clarke, as well as things for children and chaps. Accessories receive special attention, as Sheila is a stickler for detail and highly regarded by film and television companies for her historical accuracy. Handbags include the famed Hermès 'bucket' model, as well as numbers in Lucite or wicker, and Cardin classics from his 'Space Age' collection. These can all be twinned with shoes by Ferragamo, natty boots or original 1920s loafers, as well as a range of costume jewellery.

Perhaps most extraordinary of all is the collection of fabrics. Sheila has long been fascinated by materials and the ways we use them, and her stock extends to patchwork quilts, swatches, trimmings, feathers, braids, lace and ribbons of every kind. The range of textures, weights and weaves is an education, and a visit is guaranteed to deepen one's appreciation of costume and textile design.

WESTBOURNE PARK

J ane Appleby opened her eponymous shop in 2003, and only immaculate items make it on to her rails. It's no surprise to discover that today's leading designers are among the many customers who visit her for inspiration and the benefits of her unfailing eye. What they find is a hugely varied selection of vintage

Appleby

Address: 95 Westbourne Park Villas, W2
Hours: Tues–Sat 12:00–18:00 (+ Mondays, by appointment)
Telephone: 020 7229 7772 / 0780 3161 956
Tube/rail: Royal Oak
Bus: 36

womenswear full of colour, interest and surprise (with occasional titbits for the guys). An amazing Azagury evening dress rubs sequins with a 1950s full-length ball gown billowing yards of jet-black tulle, whilst a 1960s pink silk chiffon number by Hartnell makes the perfect match for a cardigan by Bill Gibb. Label-hunters risk overexcitement with the likes of a Ted Lapidus coat, a ruffle-fronted shirt by 'Granny Takes a Trip', or jackets and skirts from Lee Bender's 'Bus Stop'. Meanwhile a vibrant 1950s sun-dress by Horrockses not only looks utterly contemporary, but reminds us of the days when that illustrious name meant more than duvet covers (someone take the company over *please*!). Also making the grade are one-off ethnic items featuring feathers, embroidery or little knots of beads – just the sort of thing Nureyev might have worn about the house. There are shoes too, by the likes of Magli, Tiffany and Charles Jourdan. Dates centre round the 1940s to the 1970s, but are infinitely flexible if the individual piece is right.

The shop itself is in a shi-shi little enclave at the end of Westbourne Park Villas, the off-piste to Portobello's main run. The lighting is excellent, and the space, though not huge, entirely free of clutter or distraction. Prices reflect the impeccable quality of the clothes on offer (so expect to pay several hundred pounds for a spectacular dress, and £100+ for the shoes). For those on a limited budget it's worth noting that Jane also supplies the superb 'Vintage Princess' range at Top Shop.

Only the best

Notting Hill's two most extraordinary record shops have long been satisfying a huge range of musical tastes. While 60s fans are especially well looked after, so too are rockers, dreads, punks and jazz-buffs.

NOTTING HILL

Intoxica's own flyers tell it like it is: 'Two floors packed full of jazz, film soundtracks, blues, 60s soul, rock & roll, rhythm & blues, latin, hardcore, punk, surf, psych, beat, girl groups, 70s funk, hip hop, reggae, ska, weird & wonderful exotica, and much, much more!!!' And that very nearly sums it up — though they forgot to mention the neat Tiki Bar styling of the main room as you enter. Tribal faces stand guard over EPs by the Pretty Things and The Kinks, whilst the palm-fringed counter would not look out of place in downtown Bora Bora. Even the central light fitting is a neat little native canoe, well stocked with miniatures of rum and tequila (all the work of Josh Collins, who also decked out the wonderful South London Pacific).

Intoxica

Address: 231 Portobello Rd, London W11
Hours: Mon–Sat 10:30–18:30, Sun 12:00–17:00
Telephone: 020 7229 8010
Web: www.intoxica.co.uk
Tube/rail: Ladbroke Grove
Bus: 7, 70

This unique store is a shrine to all the low-down, dirty, garage rock'n'roll you've ever heard of – and a whole lot more besides. It's a place where Richard Berry will always be No 1, and a huge signed poster of the MC5 hangs like an altarpiece before every new worshipper who comes through the door. If 'Louie, Louie' were a shop, then this would be it: one look at the items on the walls will tell you that customers include some serious cases of vinyl addiction. Anywhere offering the South African release of The Who's *Pictures of Lily* (£400), or the Swedish edition of *Kick out the Jams* (£250) is clearly performing a valuable social service. For less acute cases there are singles by Mouse & The Traps, The Syn, Yesterday's Children,

Mambo to MC5 at everybody's favourite Tiki-styled
record shop, Intoxica

The Very Best of
BETTY EVERETT

WITH SPECIAL GUEST
APPEARANCES OF
JERRY BUTLER

A Northern Soul favourite

and thousands of LPs, both original and reissued (at six to eight pounds). Downstairs is a danger zone for those whose taste extends to jazz (check out the huge Sun Ra section), soul, 1950s rock'n'roll and blues. On the day I realized that I simply *had* to buy an album by Washboard Sam (you know the feeling) this is where I came: and I didn't go home disappointed.

Also on offer are multifarious music mags – not just the usual *Mojo*, but also superb, often quite mad 'zines such as Barracuda, Ugly Things, Cool & Strange Music, and of course Ptolemaic Terrascope! Andy, Andrea and Nick will play you things you want to hear — within reason — and generally make you feel at home (as any good doctor should). Pretty soon you'll be one of the ones standing at the counter saying: 'I don't care about the price. I *need* it!'

T wo shops for the price of one, Minus Zero and Stand Out occupy the same room just off Portobello Road, and constitute a treasure trove of rock and pop from the 60s and 70s. Joint owners are the two Bills – Forsyth and Allerton – who face each other across a narrow space for customers, and are engaged in a permanent

Minus Zero & Stand Out

Address: 2 Blenheim Crescent, London W11
Hours: Fridays & Saturdays only, 10:00–18:30
Telephone: Minus Zero 020 7229 5424; Stand Out 020 7727 8406
Web: www.minuszerorecords.com
Tube/Rail: Ladbroke Grove
Bus: 7, 70

but friendly arms race to offer the best and rarest that money can buy. Their stock does overlap but Stand Out wins the prize for 60s punk and garage whilst Minus Zero has a superb selection of folk and more melodic 1960s/1970s rock.

The place is a music junkie's paradise, where a request for something by Les Fleurs de Lys is met with: 'Do you mean the English or the *Swedish* Fleur de Lys?' Meanwhile, regulars drop by in a steady stream to discuss Wimple Winch demos or to sell LPs by The Downliners Sect. Among the current once-in-a-lifetime rarities Minus Zero has 'Mr Farmer', the first single by Thin Lizzie (note the spelling). This was an Irish-only release and probably no more than a couple of hundred were ever produced. The 'guide' price of £1000 probably underestimates the sum a collector will eventually pay! For its part, Stand Out boasts a one-off acetate by Bob Dylan with hand-written label stating 'I Will Be *Relieved*' (rather than 'Released'!) and originally given to Manfred Mann in the hope that they'd cover it and bring in some royalties. After those two items, the Japanese EPs by the Who or Iggy Pop seem almost commonplace.

But it's not all super-rare stuff. Thousands of CDs averaging £12 each will allow you to explore every imaginable by-way of post-1950s, pre-1980s pop and rock. The reissued LPs are also worth investigating, including the latest gems from label Akarma, which is on a mission to bring back forgotten prog-rock albums in all their gatefold-sleeved glory. The building itself has quite a story to tell, having once been the 'Dog House', one of London's first and most famous 'head shops' as well as being the UK outpost of legendary 1960s West Coast poster-designers 'The Family Dog' (you'll even see the Blenheim Crescent address on some of their work). Bill and Bill will play you anything you ask to hear, and are happy to impart their great and priceless wisdom.

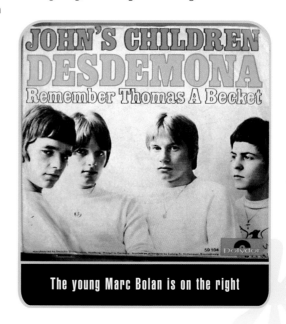

The young Marc Bolan is on the right

west: wheels

Ealing guards its secrets well – but not well enough! Twin legends of the British Bike and Kustom Kar worlds both have their HQs off the main drag. Further West in Greenford, the London Motorcycle Museum boasts a priceless line-up of prototypes and works racers.

EALING

What a great name! – and one that's lived up to. For well over a decade, this unique Classic Car Restorer has been drawing clued-up enthusiasts to the backstreets of Ealing, unlikeliest of homes to one of London's undisputed Crown Jewels of Cool.

The business is the brainchild of master metalworker Lance McCormack, who many will recognize from his regular appearances on Channel 4's *Salvage Squad*. He received his training at Rolls Royce's famed Mulliner Park-Ward site, where he had the good fortune to be one of the last generation of professional coach builders. He also had the natural-born talent to become their youngest-ever final inspector. Whilst he turns his hand to other marques these days, they all receive the same unstinting care and attention.

The cars themselves are nothing short of jaw-dropping. On a typical day the workshop is home to an amazing array of Le Mans winners, silver-screen gems and radically customized Big Yank Tin. Chief among the Kustoms – or 'lead sleds' – is Lance's very own set of wheels, affectionately known as 'Planet Voodoo'. What began life as a 1950 Ford Mercury now boasts a V8 motor from a 1957 Lincoln Continental and an interior that has to be seen to be believed. The steering wheel and gauges are embellished with boa constrictor skin and 'toons hand-painted by the master of retro erotica, Vince Ray. Regularly featured in Hot

Romance of Rust

Address: Phoenix House, St Helen's Rd, Ealing, W13
Hours: Phone to confirm
Telephone: 020 8840 8144 / 07774 754239
Web: www.romanceofrust.co.uk
Tube/rail: West Ealing
Bus: 83, 207, E2, E7, E8, E11

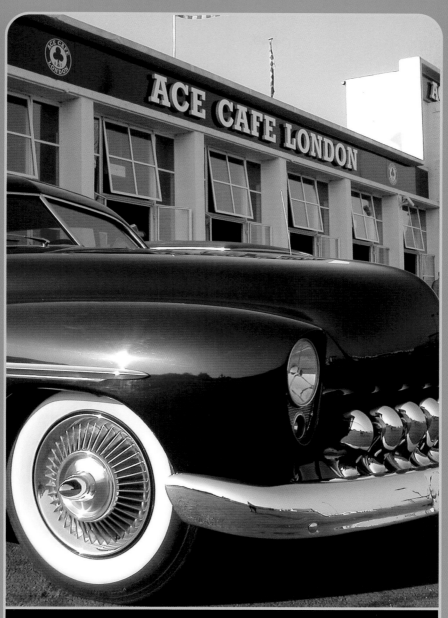

A lead-sled like no other, the prize-winning 'Planet Voodoo' takes a
pit stop at the Ace

Rod and classic car magazines the world over, 'Planet Voodoo' can often be found at the Ace Café, where Lance also happened to build the bar.

As for the non-customized vehicles at Romance, none of them is exactly the kind one sees everyday. Recently in for treatment was a near-mythical Facel-Vega which arrived directly from Las Vegas and was once the runabout of Ava Gardner. There are Jaguar XK140s, Ford Galaxies and DB5s. Even what looks at first like an ordinary VW Beetle turns out to have once belonged to Keith Moon.

Romance's customers are an improbable mix. Blue-blooded city types come to maintain the family 'stable' of historic British racers, whilst rock'n'rollers with cash and attitude tend to own the chrome and fins. For their inimitable work, Lance and his team charge around £40 per hour, plus VAT. The amount spent on a single car is simply a matter of how much work is required. Sums of more than £100,000 have been known, conjuring up the kind of radically transformed fantasy machines that compete for big prizes. Remember, there are no cars actually for sale here: customers bring the metal, and Lance supplies the sweat and genius to realize their dreams.

Reg Allen is one of West London's hidden retro gems. Since opening this shop in Hanwell almost 50 years ago, owner Bill Crosby has been a torch-bearer par excellence for the once-proud British bike industry. He's been around, as he puts it, 'from the golden age to the rusty age', and the machines he once sold new in the 1950s are now in demand again as the timeless classics they are universally acknowledged to be.

To come here is to commune with the whole

Reg Allen

Address: 39–41 Grosvenor Rd, Hanwell, W7
Hours: Mon–Fri 09:30-19:00, Sat 09:30-18:00
Telephone: 020 8579 1248
Web: www.reg-allen-london.20m.com
Tube/rail: Hanwell/West Ealing
Bus: 83, 207, E3, E8

ALSO: London Motorcycle Museum
Address: Ravenor Farm, 29 Oldfield Lane South, Greenford, Middlesex
Hours: Weekends & Bank Holidays 10:00-16:30
Telephone: 020 8575 6644
Web: www.london-motorcycle-museum.org
Tube/rail: Greenford
Bus: E1, E2, E6, E7, E10, 92, 105

history of British biking, of which Bill himself is an integral part. He launched the London Motorcycle Museum some five years ago, after a prodigious effort, and the building in nearby Greenford now shelters 70 to 80 bikes, including many unique prototypes and 'works racers'. The collection has become even more important following the tragic fire that all but destroyed the National Bike Museum in Birmingham in 2003. Best of all, only a short strip of motorway separates Greenford from the Ace Café, which makes for a perfect combination.

Incredibly, it's new!

The shop itself is a true time capsule, where the shelves are stacked high with parts for long-discontinued vehicles, and the walls are plastered with posters and ads from a simpler, pre-decimal era. Most of the bikes in stock are Triumphs from the company's famed Meridian plant, though they are frequently joined by other Brit-built legends such as an all-original 1936 Velocette complete with girder forks and bicycle-style saddle.

Prices are extremely reasonable, with popular vehicles such as the Triumph T150 or T160 selling for around £2,500/£3,000, perhaps a little more for something truly outstanding. Customers these days are often commuters attracted by the convenience and style of a classic British bike, along with older buyers coming to pick up models they last sat astride in the 1960s. Speed fanatics, however, tend to stick with newer rides, as the older designs were not built for modern motorway travel. The collectors' market is different again, and Triumph's legendary 'Bonnevilles' have in recent years been bid up to extraordinary values: as much as £15,000 is not unheard of, taking them sadly out of the range of ordinary users and old-style enthusiasts.

The only new bikes Bill sells are the Royal Enfields, made in India to original 1950s designs. A 350cc model goes for around £2,500, and a 500cc more like £3000, and they all look *fantastic*. What's more, they have all the reliability of a brand new machine. Time was when the Enfields from the sub-continent looked a whole lot better than they actually ran, but recent years have seen the company's new managers make a real effort to produce bikes that could hold their own in the exacting European market. The end results are irresistible!

the retro scene

How better to break in those vintage dancing shoes than at one of London's retro-friendly nightclubs. Here's a selection for rug-cutters, hip-shakers and big-groove hunters of all persuasions. Be sure to check websites for latest details or pick up the flyers at record shops

60s/70s
DIRTY WATER
North London institution at which the true spirit of rock'n'roll is invoked by a roster of neo-glam-garage-punk-psychedelic bands and a kick-ass all-eras playlist.
www.dirtywaterclub.com
Harpers Bar, The Boston, 178 Junction Rd, N19; every Friday, 20.30-03.00 (Tube: Tufnell Park)

HEAVY LOAD
Unique and unmissable monthly event devoted to early 70s rock.
www.heavyload.clara.co.uk
The Phoenix, Cavendish Square, W1; one Saturday each month, 21.00-03.00 (Tube: Oxford Circus)

60s
For latest info on 60s clubs visit:
www.newuntouchables.com
The clubs themselves are for true connoisseurs of 60s fashion and music, though anyone making the effort is welcome to join the fun.

FAB
Needles Cellar Club, 5 Clipstone St, W1; one Saturday each month, 21.30-02.00 (Tube: Gt. Portland St)

MAGICK POTION
Centro, 93 Grays Inn Rd, WC1; one Saturday each month, 22.00-03.00 (Tube: Chancery Lane)

MOUSETRAP
Orleans, 259 Seven Sisters Rd, N4; one Saturday each month, 22.00-06.00 (Tube: Finsbury Park)

6TS ALL NITER
Truly legendary club.
www.6ts.info 100 Club, 100 Oxford St, W1; one Saturday each month, usually 01.30-08.00 (Tube: Tottenham Court Rd)

CAPITOL SOUL CLUB
www.capitolsoulclub.com
The Dome, above The Boston, 178 Junction Rd, N19; last Friday every other month, 21.30-03.00 (Tube: Tufnell Park). Members only.

SHAKE
Not a members club, and free to get in!! Great for newcomers.
www.pleasureunitbar.com/shake.htm
The Pleasure Unit, 359 Bethnal Green Rd, E2; one Friday each month, 20.00-02.00 (Tube: Bethnal Green)

50s/60s
LADY LUCK
Eclectic, wild and decadent night, with live acts ranging from one-man acid blues to retro-raunch burlesque.
www.ladyluckclub.co.uk
The Millennium Club, 167 Drury Lane, WC2; every Friday, 21.00-03.00 (Tube: Covent Garden)

VIRGINIA CREEPERS
Bands range from rockers and garage punks to CBGBs-style New Wavers.
www.virginiacreepersclub.co.uk
The Water Rats, 328 Grays Inn Rd, WC1; one Saturday each month, 21.00-late, bands on stage at 10.30 (Tube: Kings Cross)

50s
TENNESSEE CLUB
Spiritual home to London's Teddy Boys, boasting live appearances by The Comets and Scotty Moore. Trent Park Golf Club, Bramley Rd, Oakwood, N14; one night most months, check website for details (Tube: Oakwood)

40s/50s/Swing Dance
HELLZAPOPPIN
Home to some of London's best swing-jivers.

www.efdss.org/this_wk.htm
Cecil Sharp House, 2 Regent's Park
Rd, NW1; one Saturday each
month, 20.00-24.00 (Tube:
Camden Town)

HULA BOOGIE

Lovely relaxed night with great
and eclectic music spun by Miss
Aloha and The Reverend Boogie.
www.southlondonpacific.com
South London Pacific, 340
Kennington Rd, SE11; last Sunday
of each month, 19.45-24.00
(Tube: Oval)

JITTERBUG BALL

Spectacular annual event
attracting a sell-out crowd from all
over the world and brought to you
by Robin & Colette, the people
behind the Jiving Jamboree. Dance
to the sounds of a live Big Band
and soak up the unique
atmosphere. Dress code is allied
uniform or 40s civilian (though
evening dress is OK too).
www.jitterbugball.com
Hammersmith Town Hall, King St,
W6; one Saturday in June, 20.30-
01.00 (Tube: Ravenscourt Park)

JITTERBUGS

Dance teacher Julie Oram's
popular weekly event, starting
with a lesson and moving on to
guest DJs and a once-a-month live
band. www.jitterbugs.co.uk
Carisbrooke Hall, 63/79 Seymour
St, W2; every Wednesday, 19.30-
23.30 (Tube: Marble Arch)

JIVING JAMBOREE

Long running and popular night
with a superb sprung dance floor
and a raised stage graced each
month by top quality live bands.
www.jivingjamboree.com
See also www.learntojive.com for
details of regular dance classes.
Ealing Town Hall, Uxbridge Rd,
W5; one Saturday each month,
20.00-00.30 (Tube: Ealing
Broadway)

STOMPIN'

Flagship event of the London
Swing Dance Society, beginning
each week with a dance lesson
and revving up later with a live
band.
www.swingdanceuk.com
100 Club, 100 Oxford St, London
W1; every Monday, lesson at 7.45,
band on at 9.15 for first of two
sets (Tube: Tottenham Court Rd.)

acknowledgements

The author would like to thank all the shop, club and café owners who gave their time for this book, along with a great deal of encouragement and advice. A particular thank you goes to Mark Wilsmore at the Ace Café, whose can-do philosophy has been an inspiration throughout. I'm also very grateful to Gordon Ayres for use of his photographs, and to Avis Judd for her excellent suggestions. And finally a big 'Honey I'm Home' to my ever-supportive wife, Charlotte.